# Fox

## Coloring Book

## Toddlers



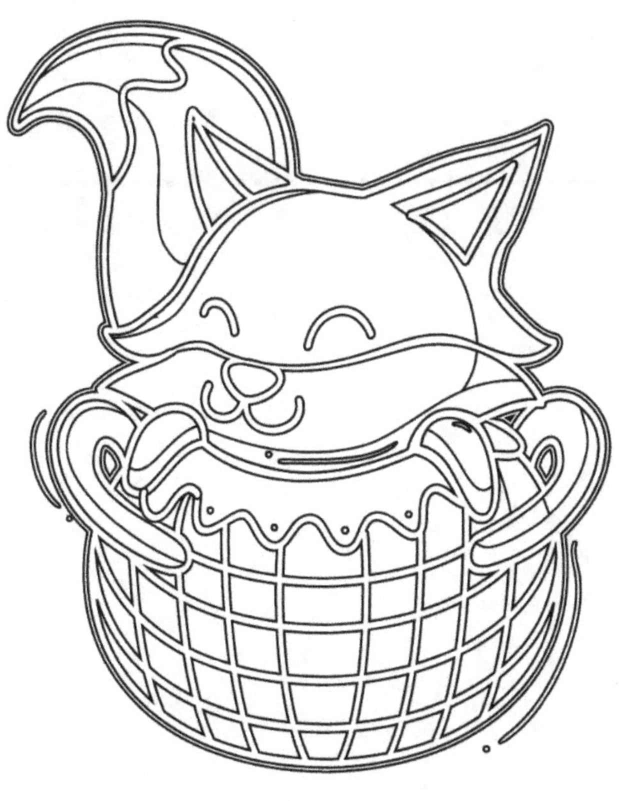

# This Book Belongs To

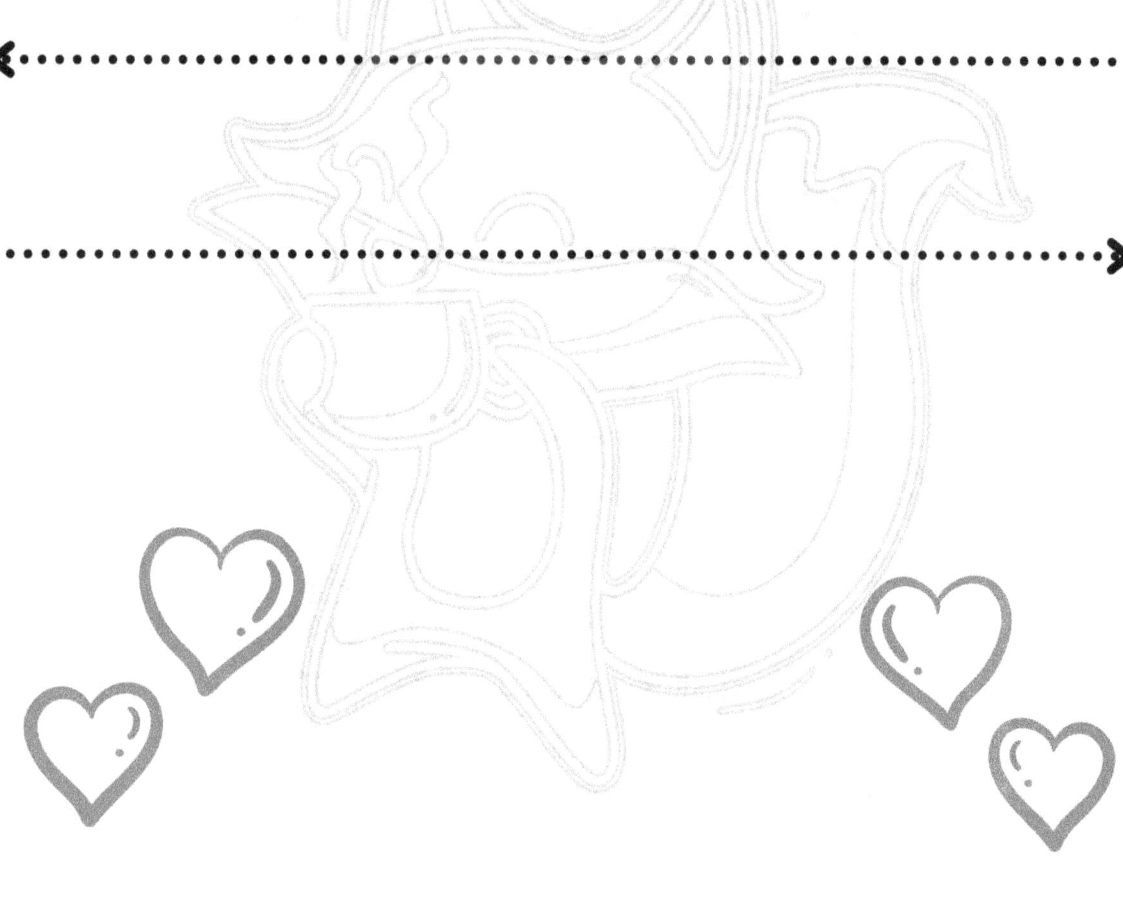

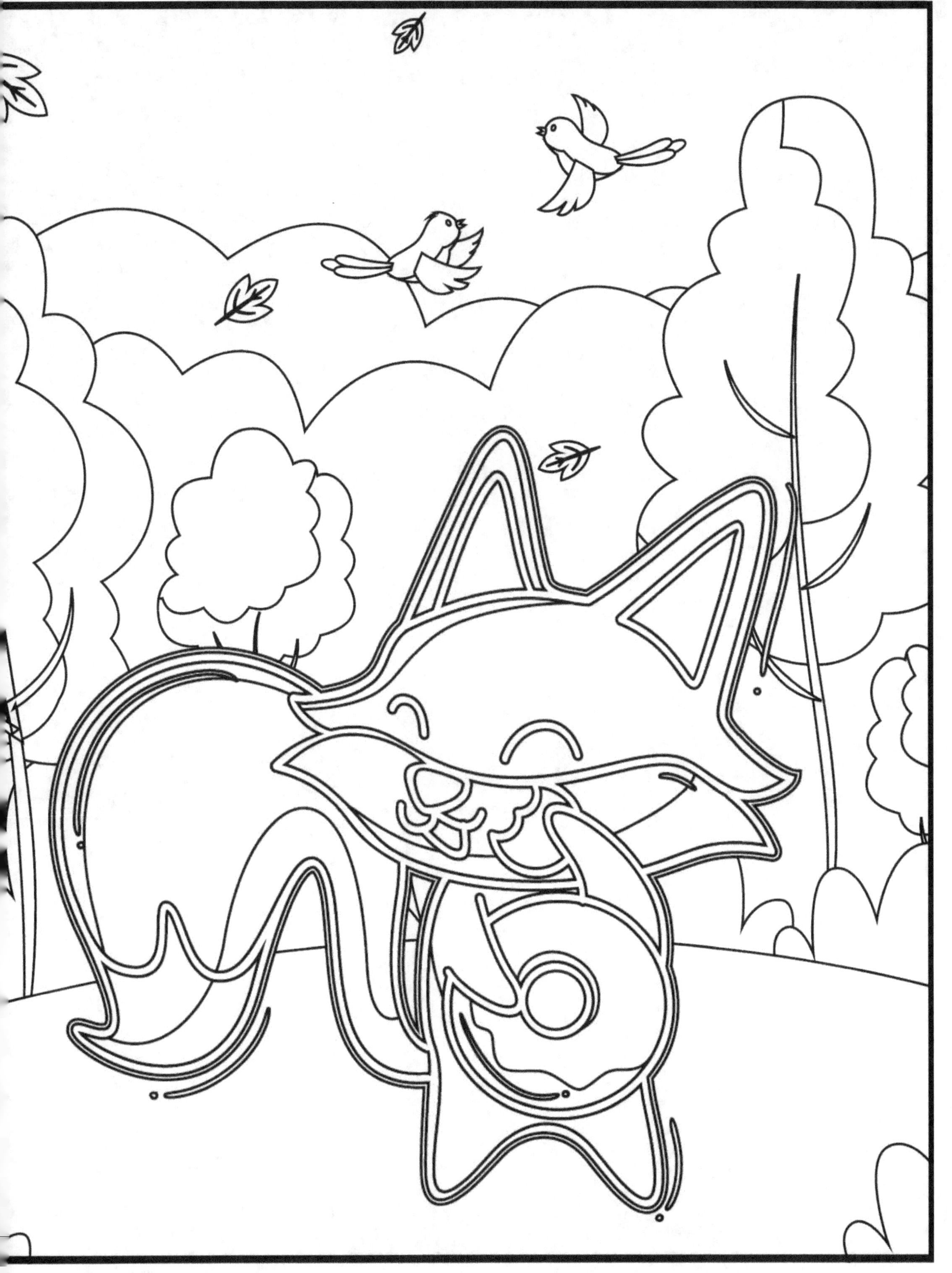

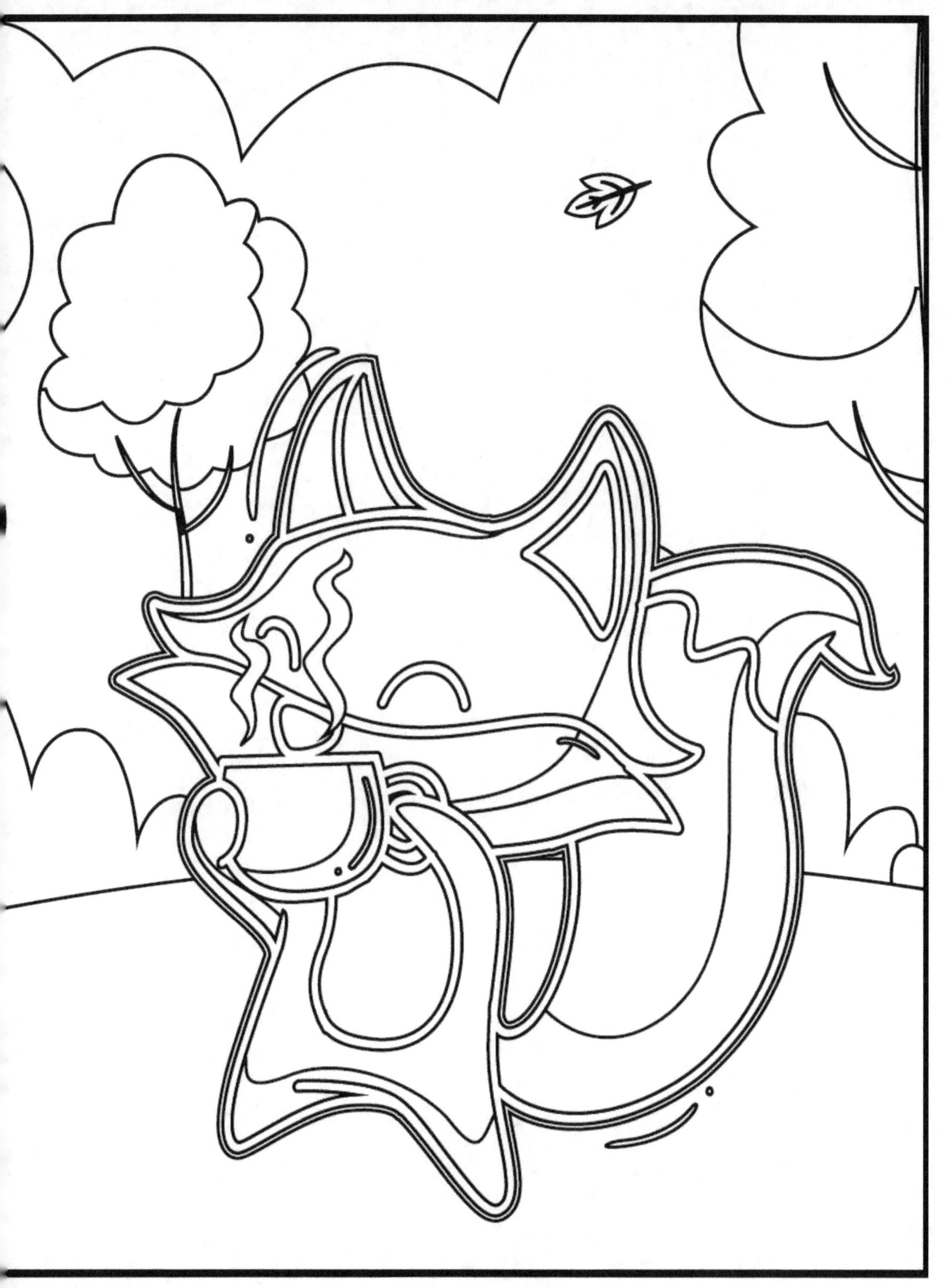

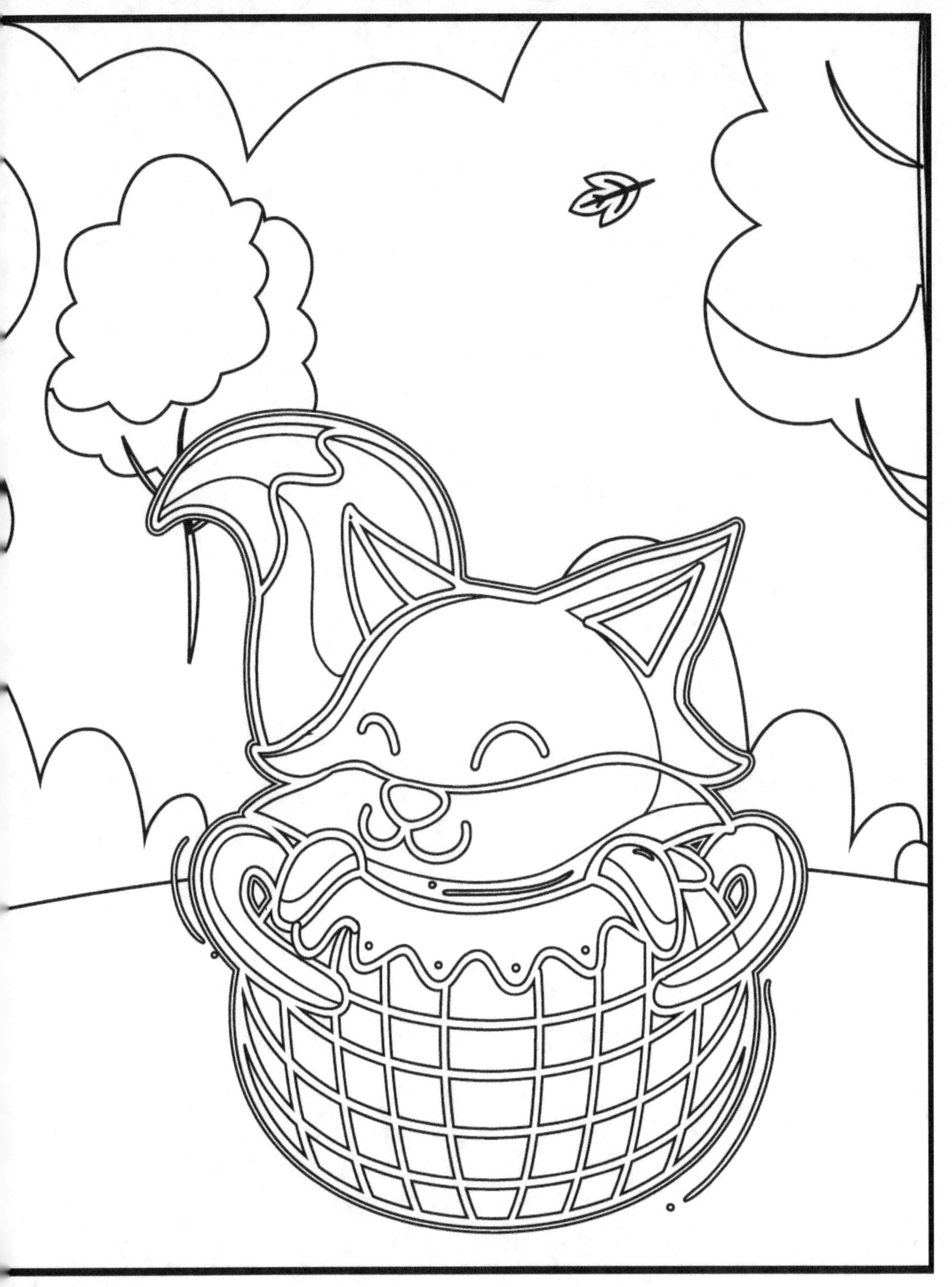

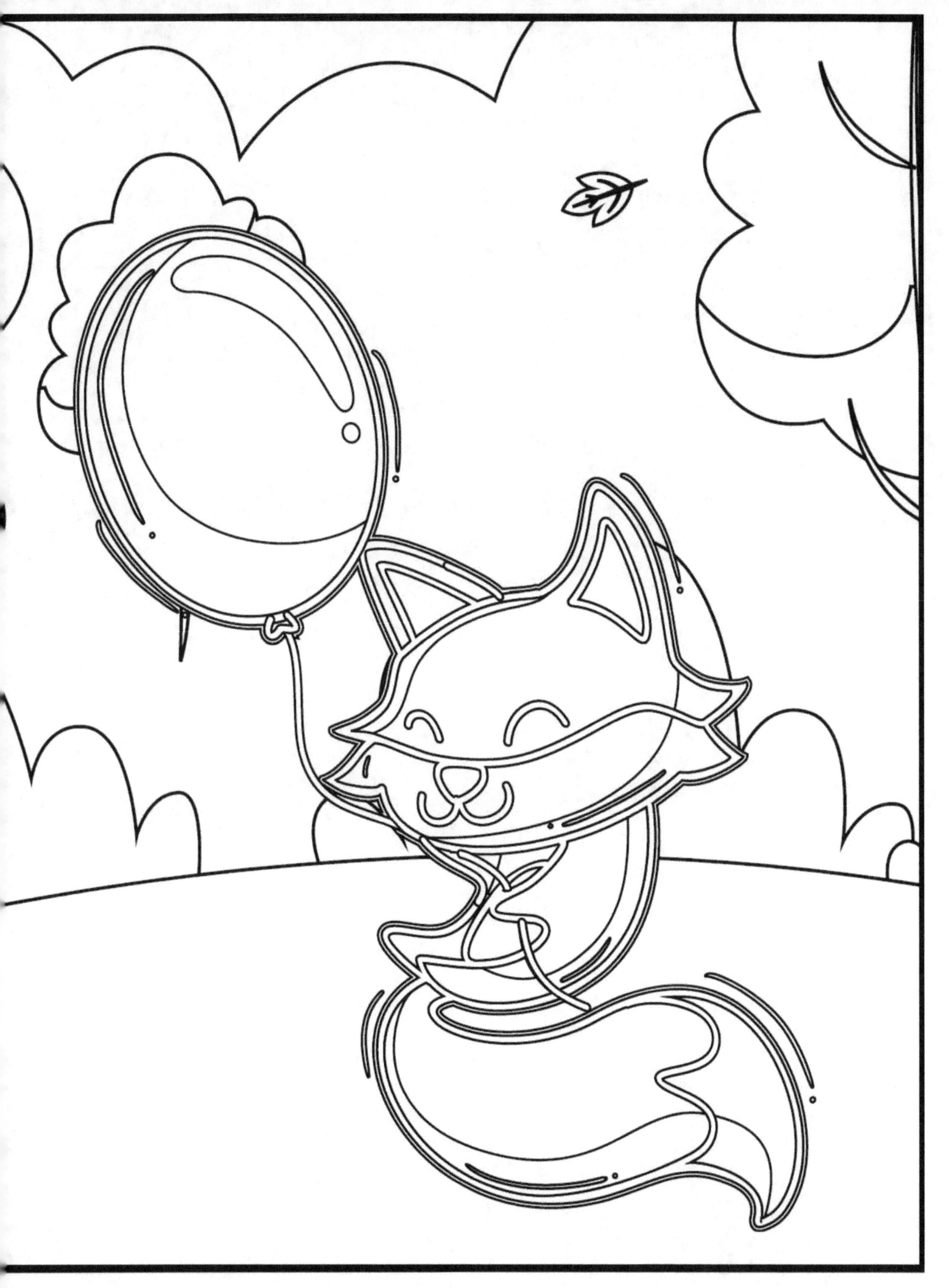

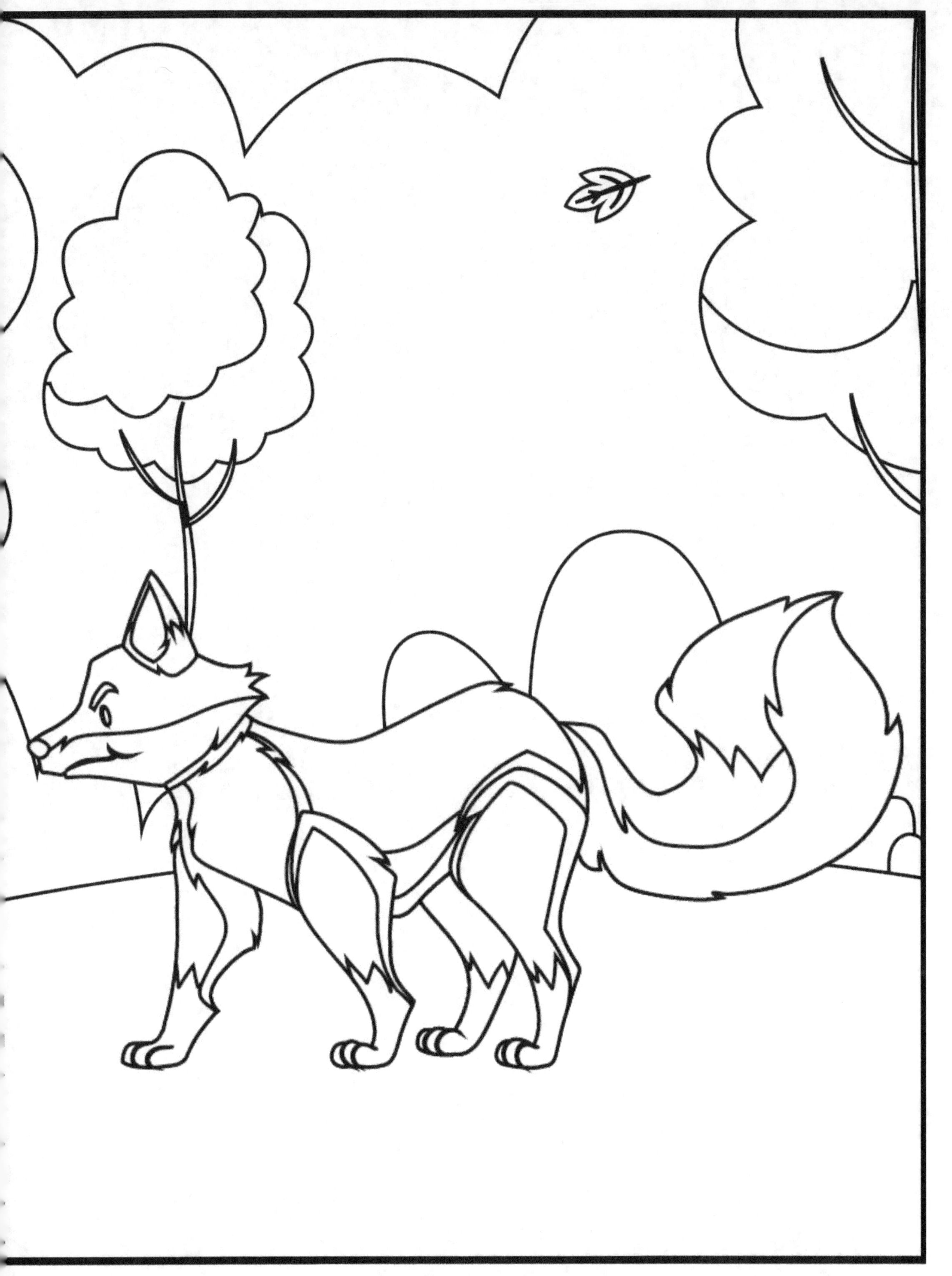

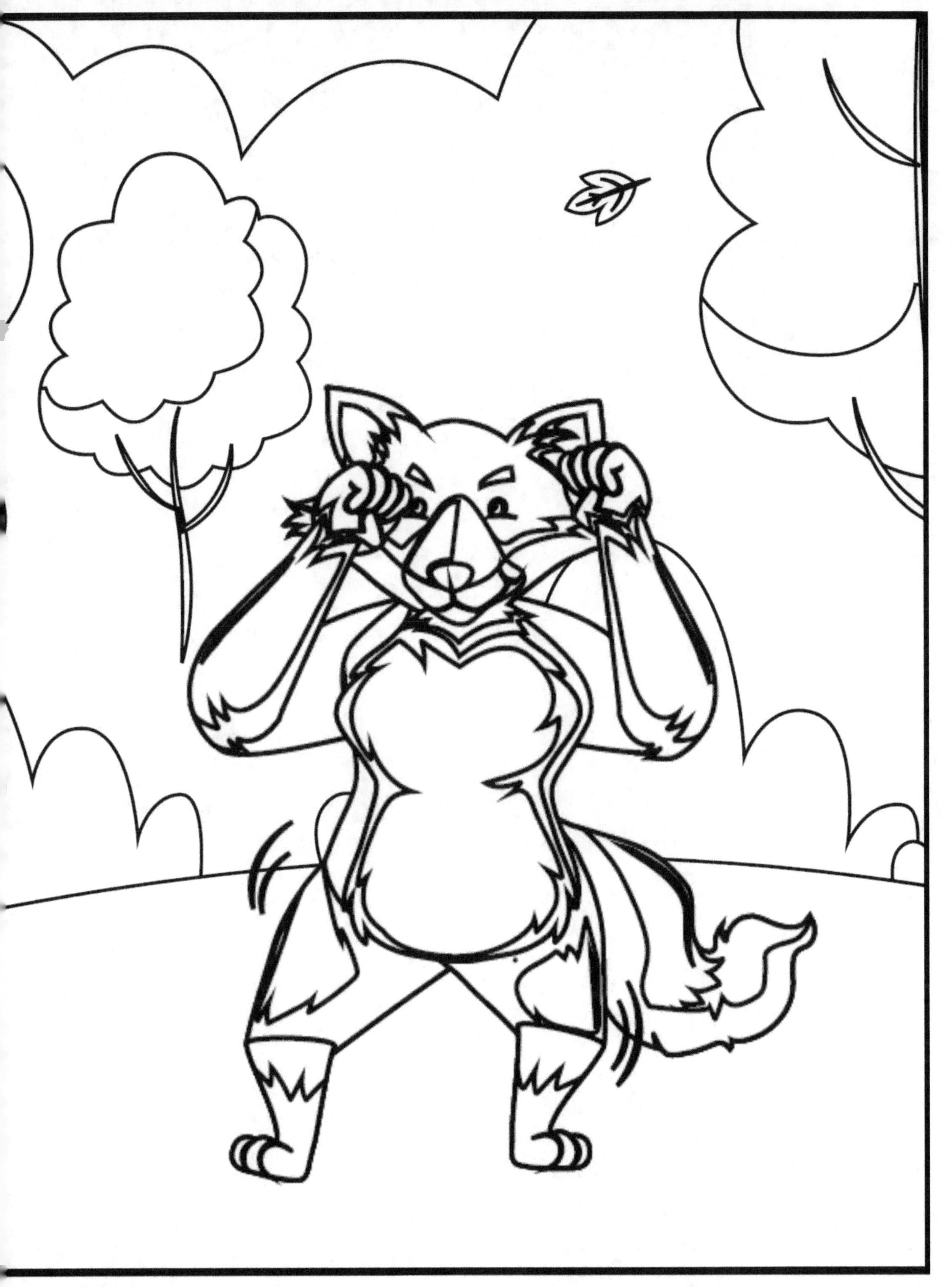

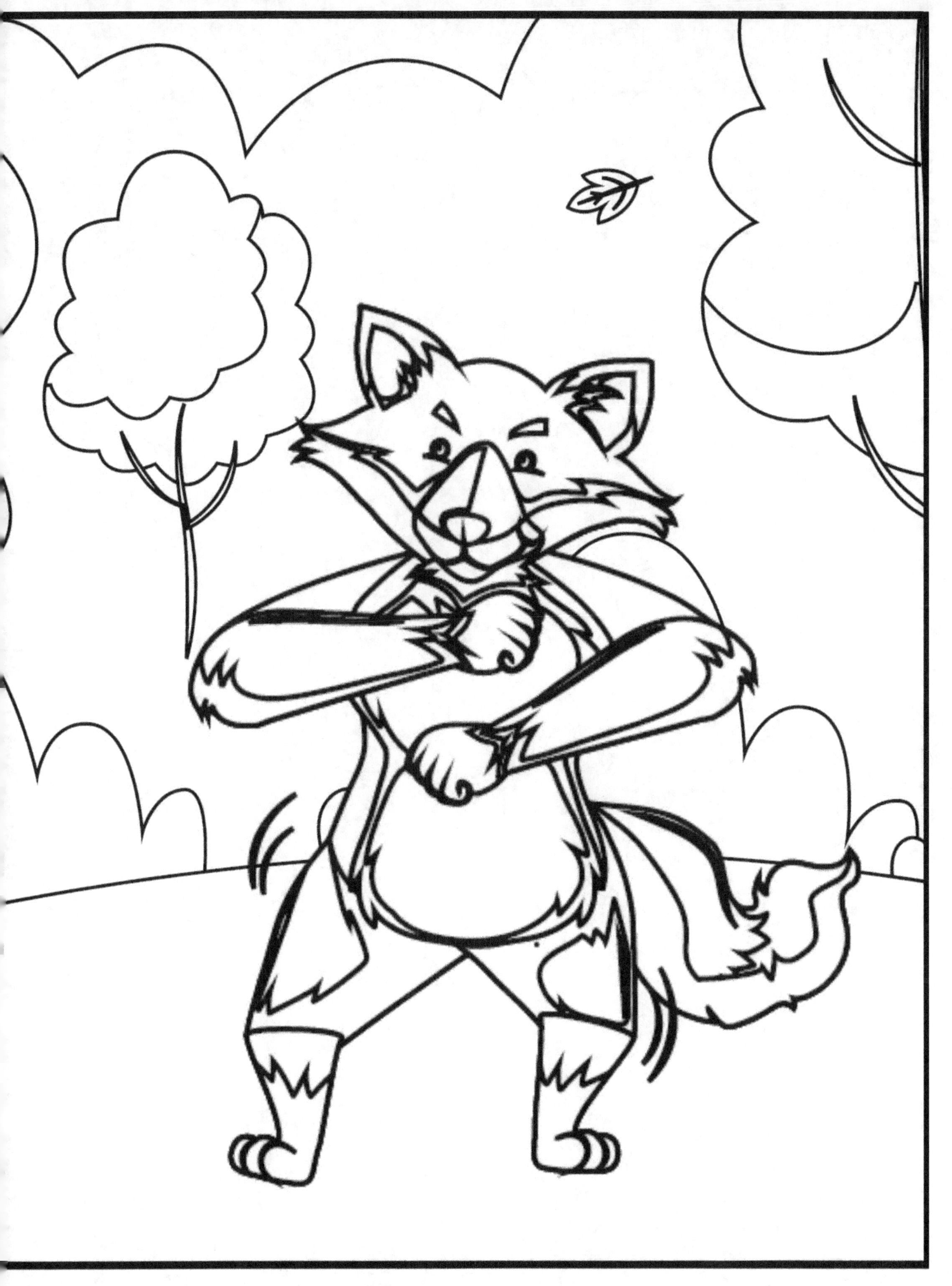

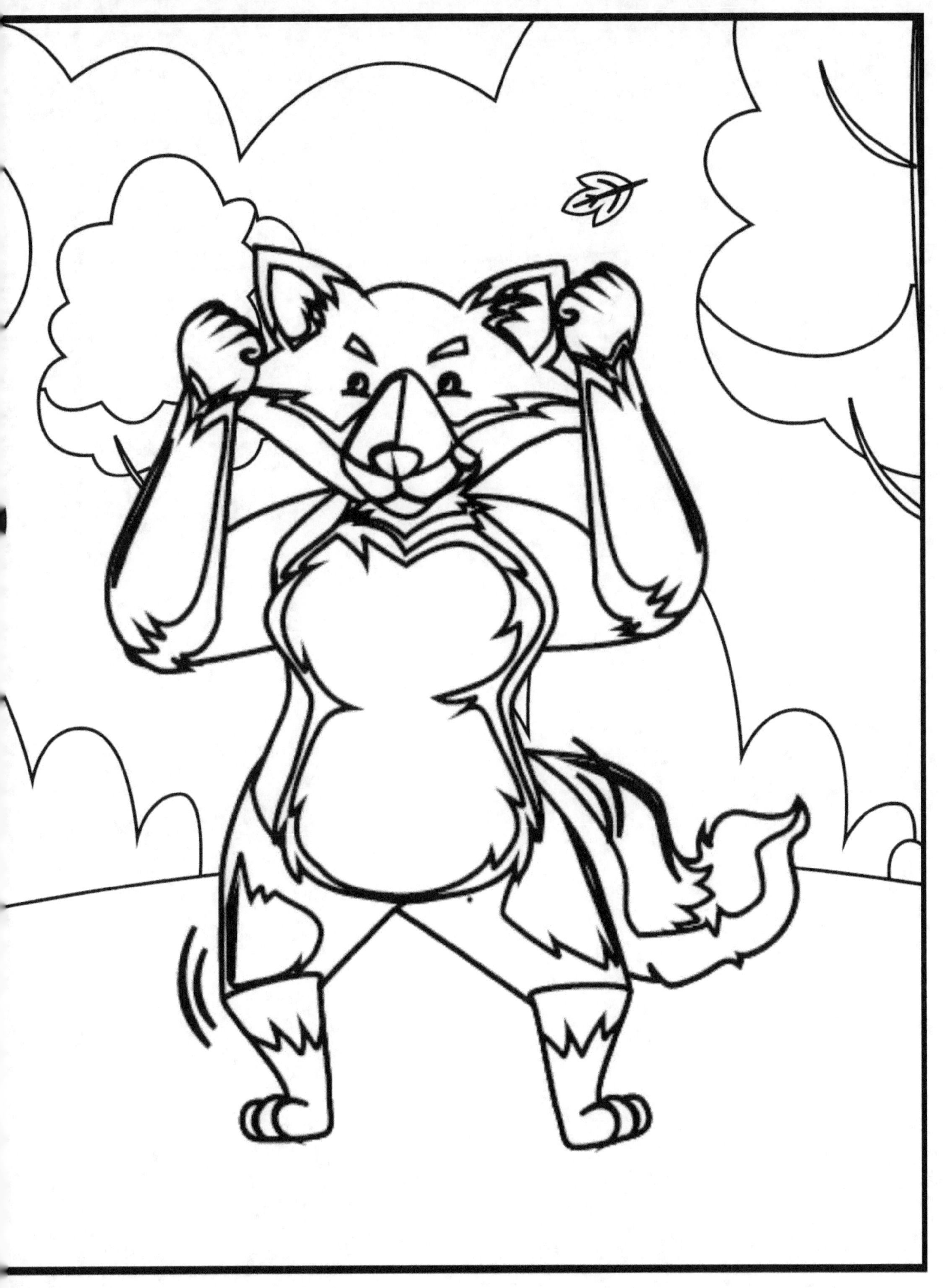

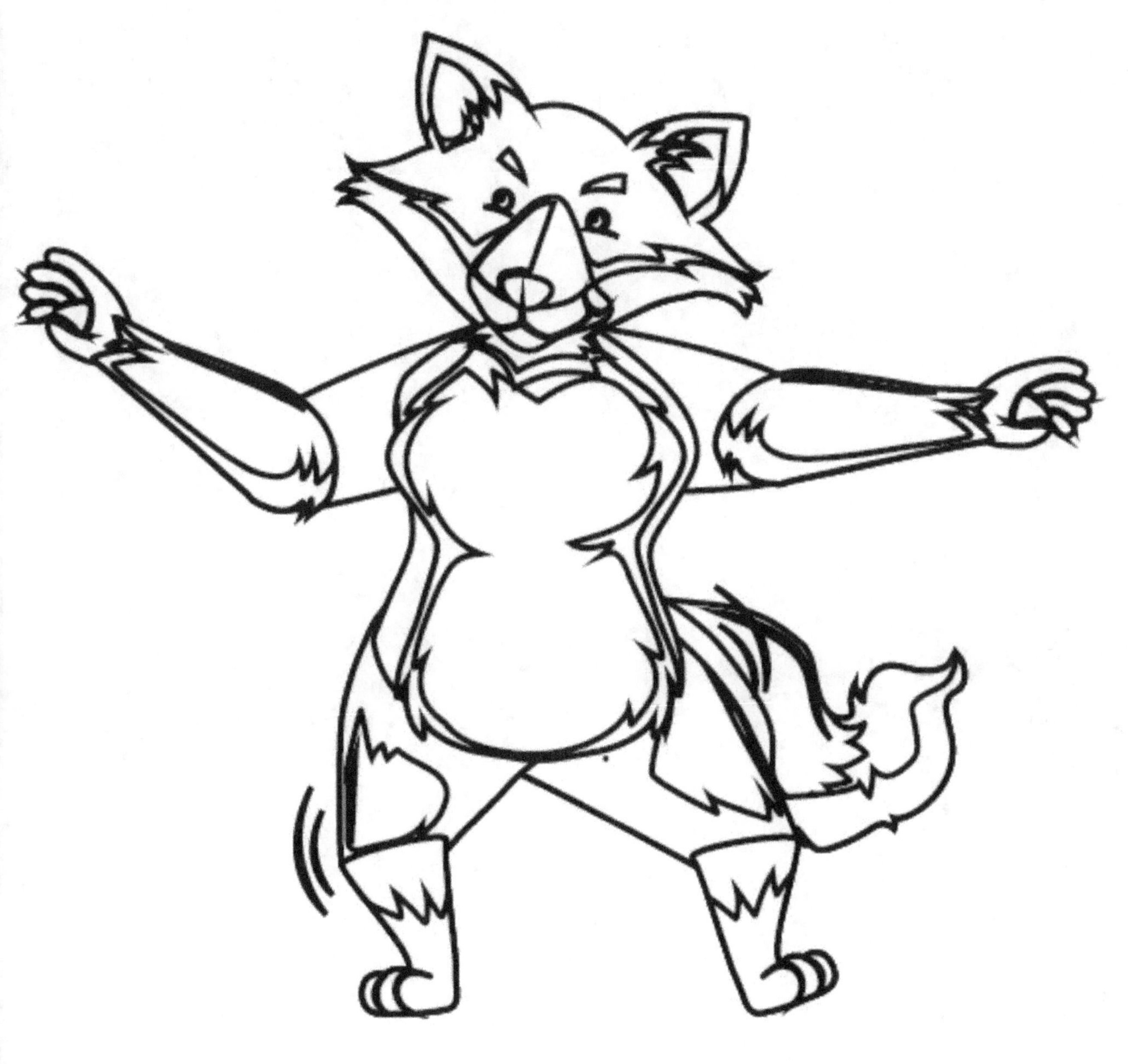

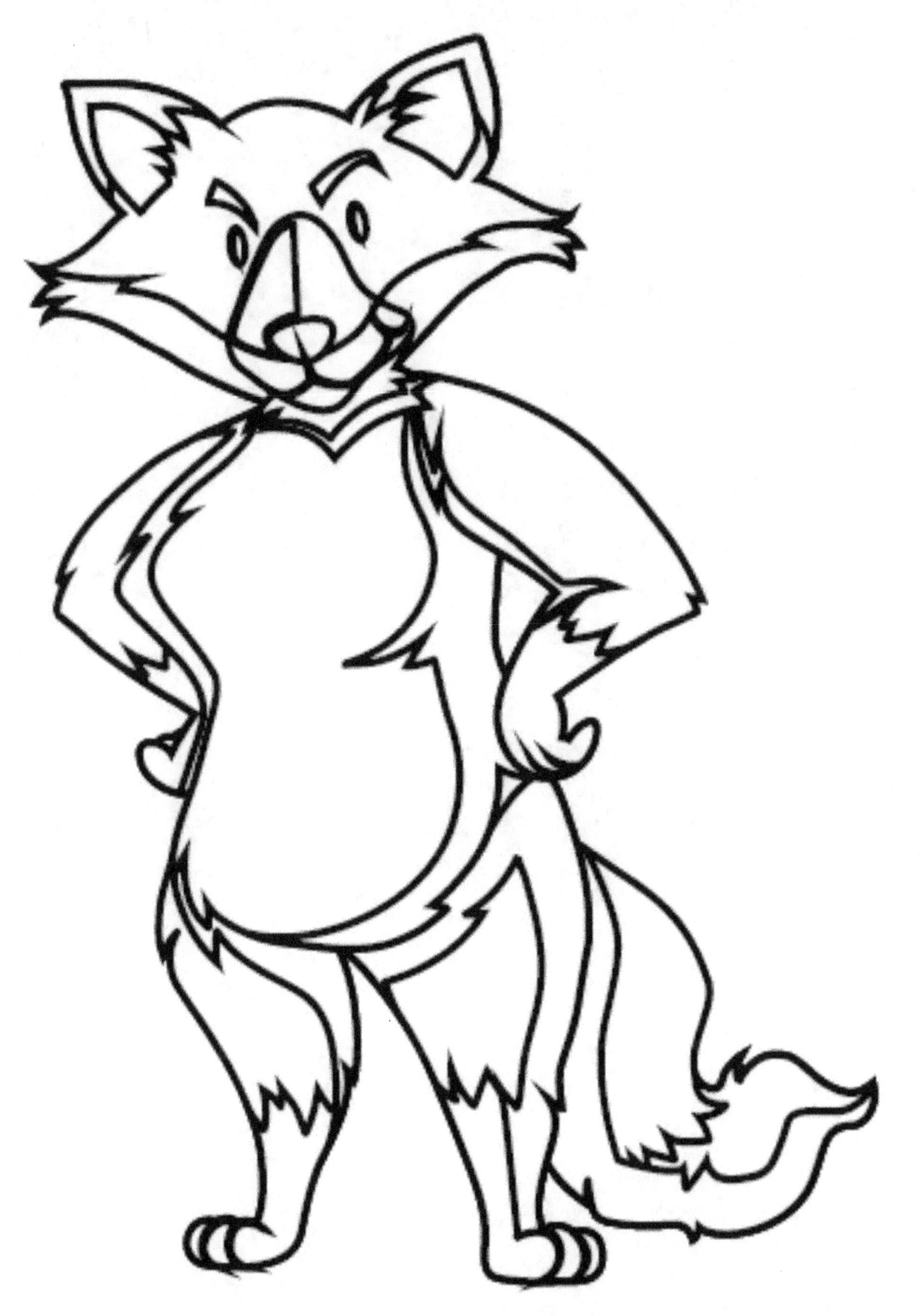

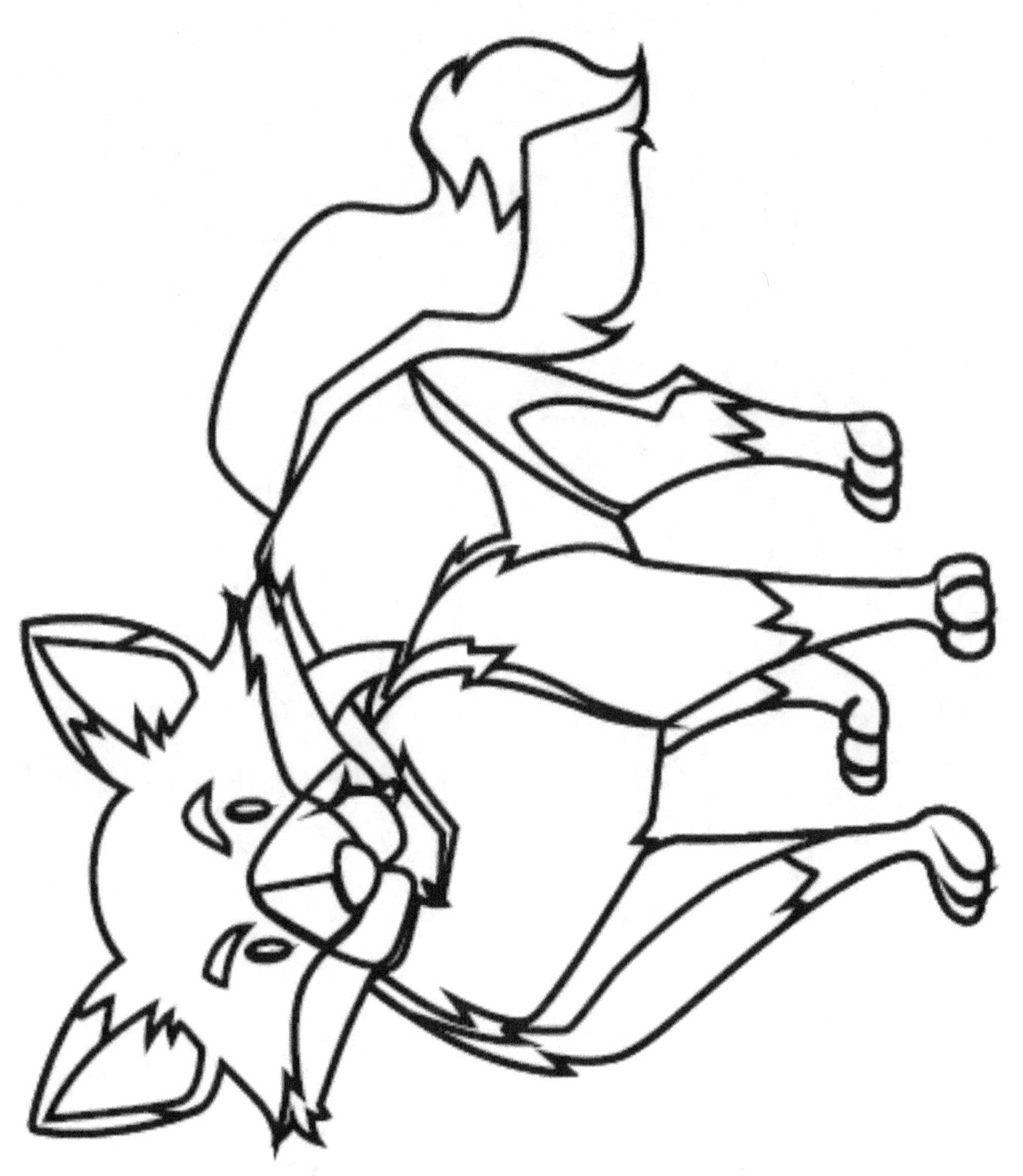

2+2=?
5x2=?
4-1=?
12/3=?

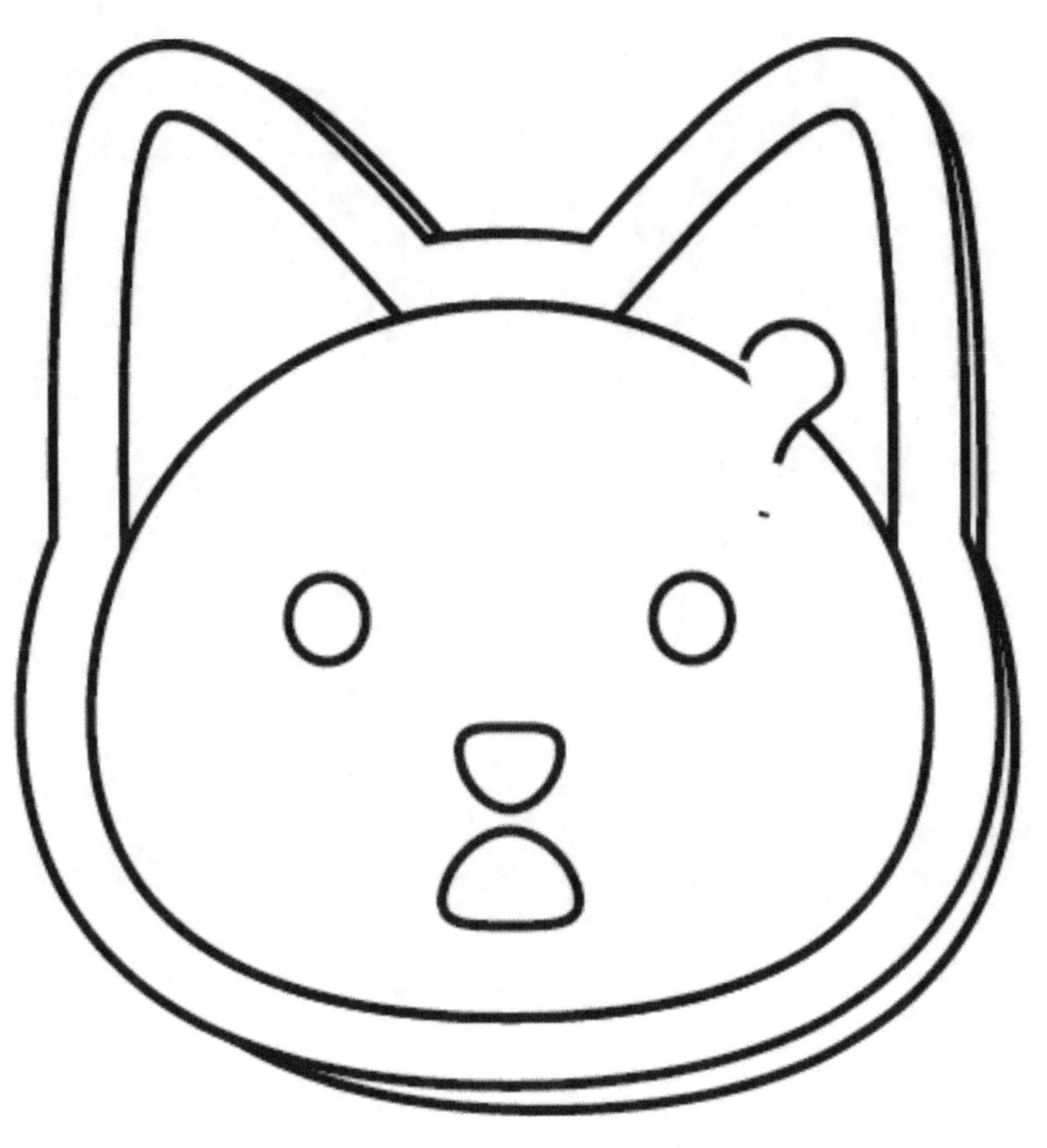

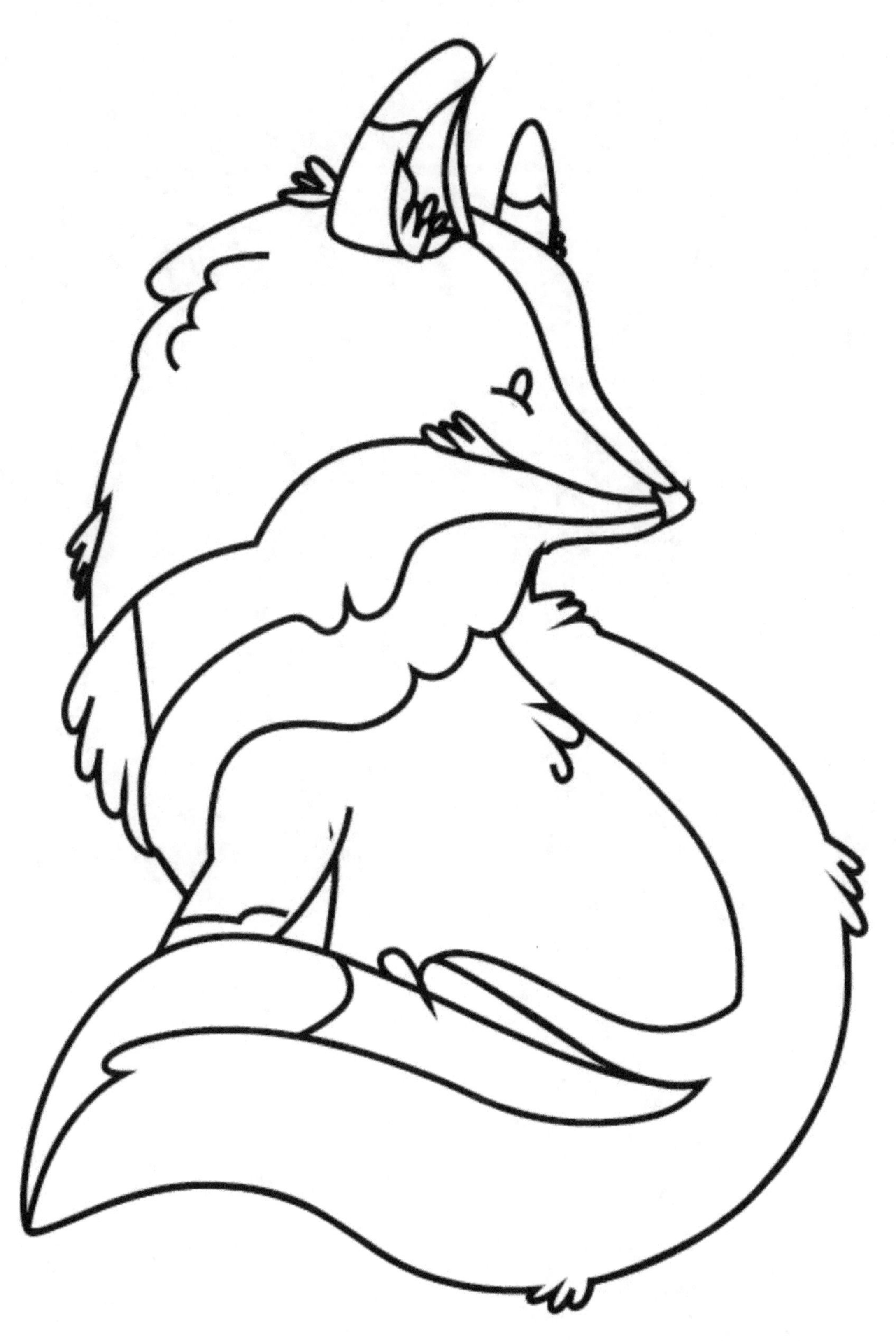

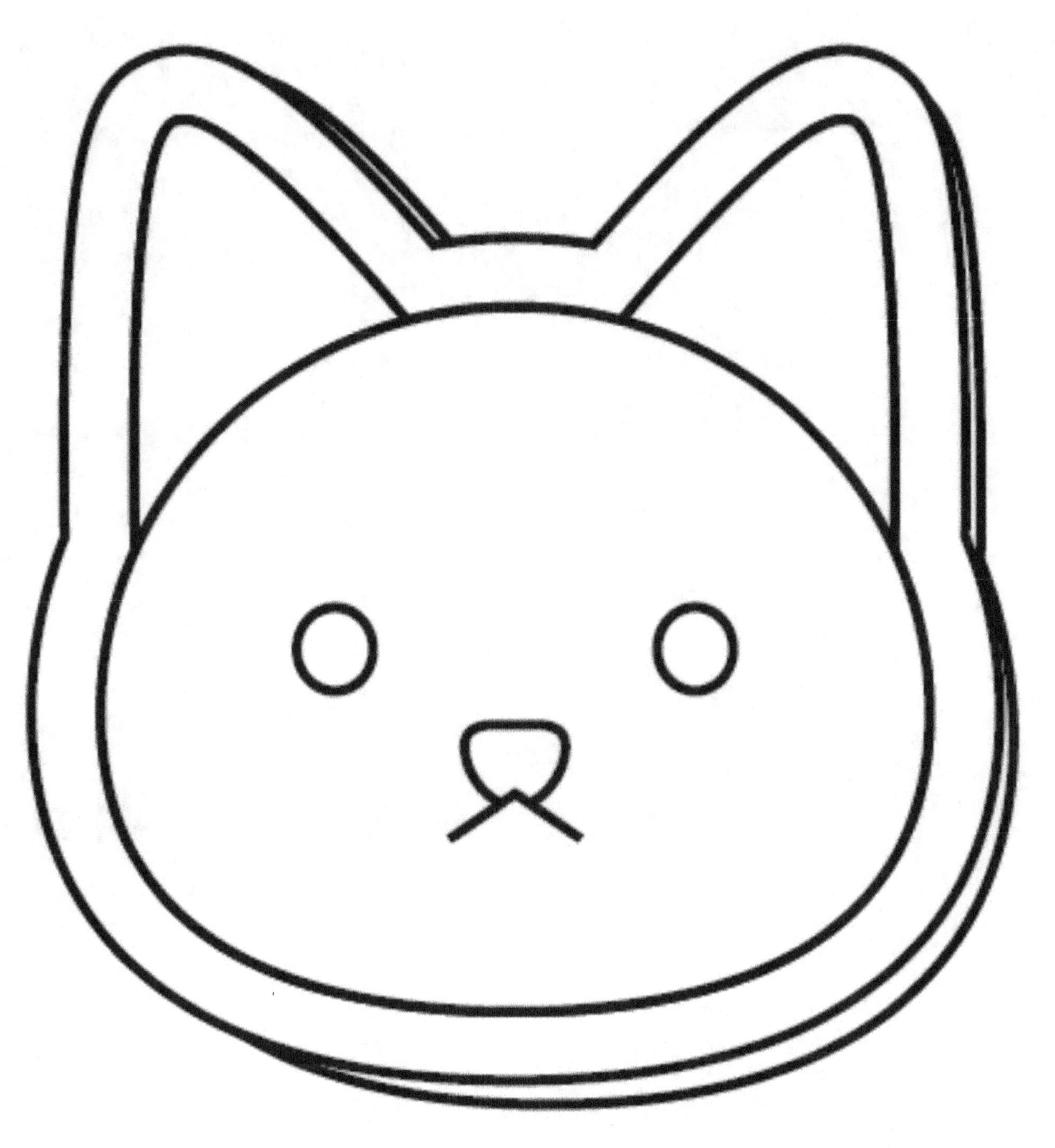

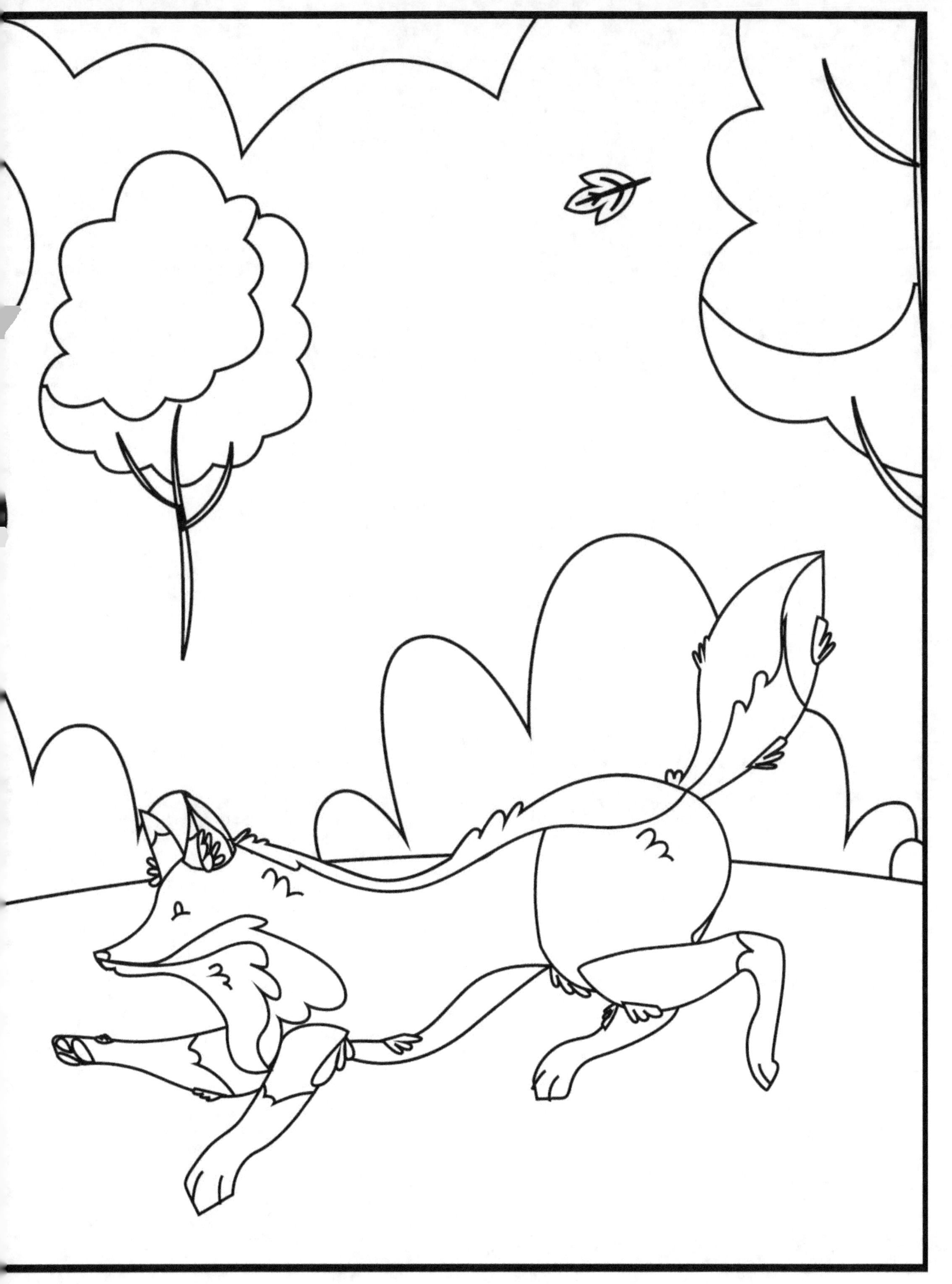

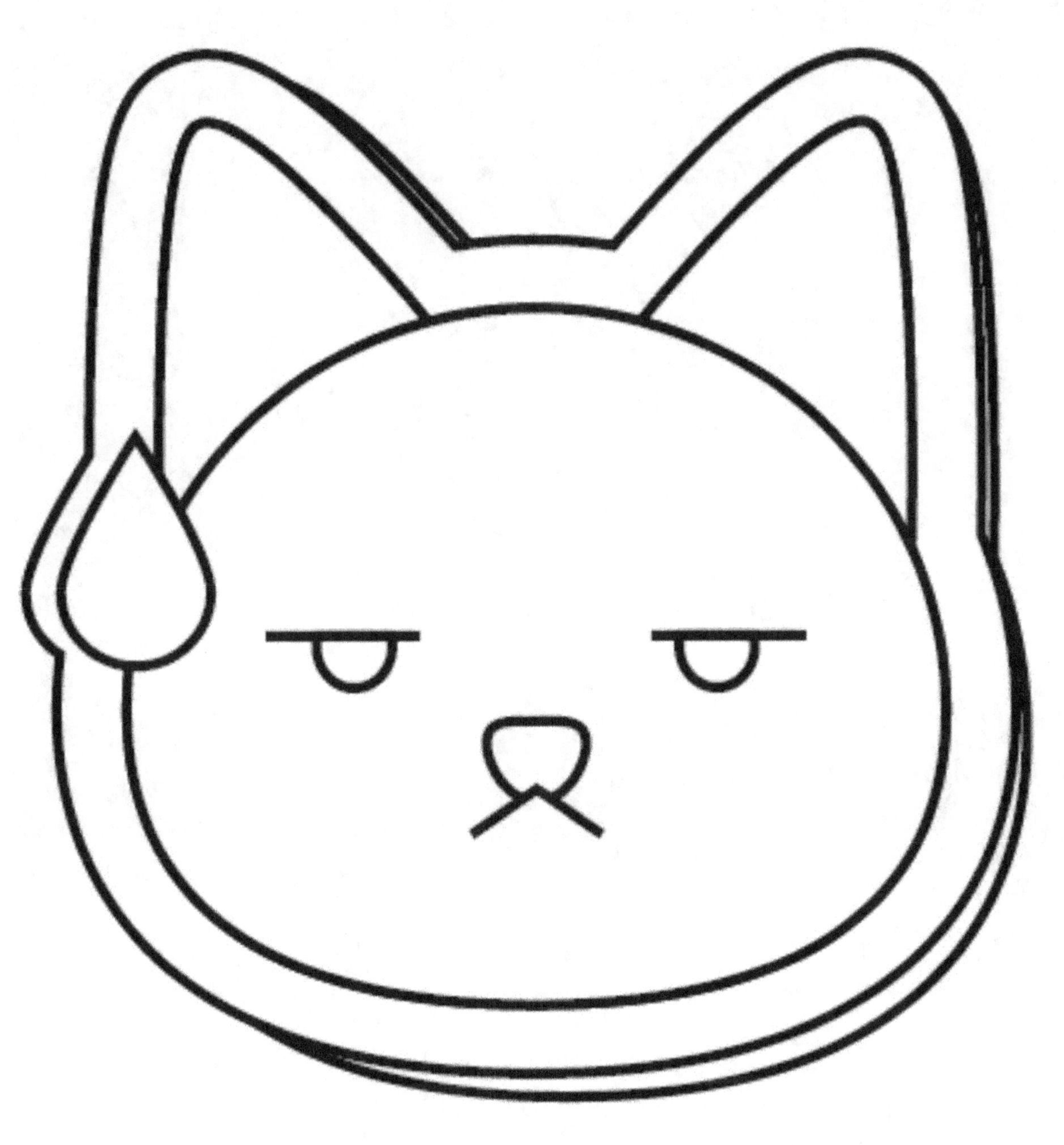

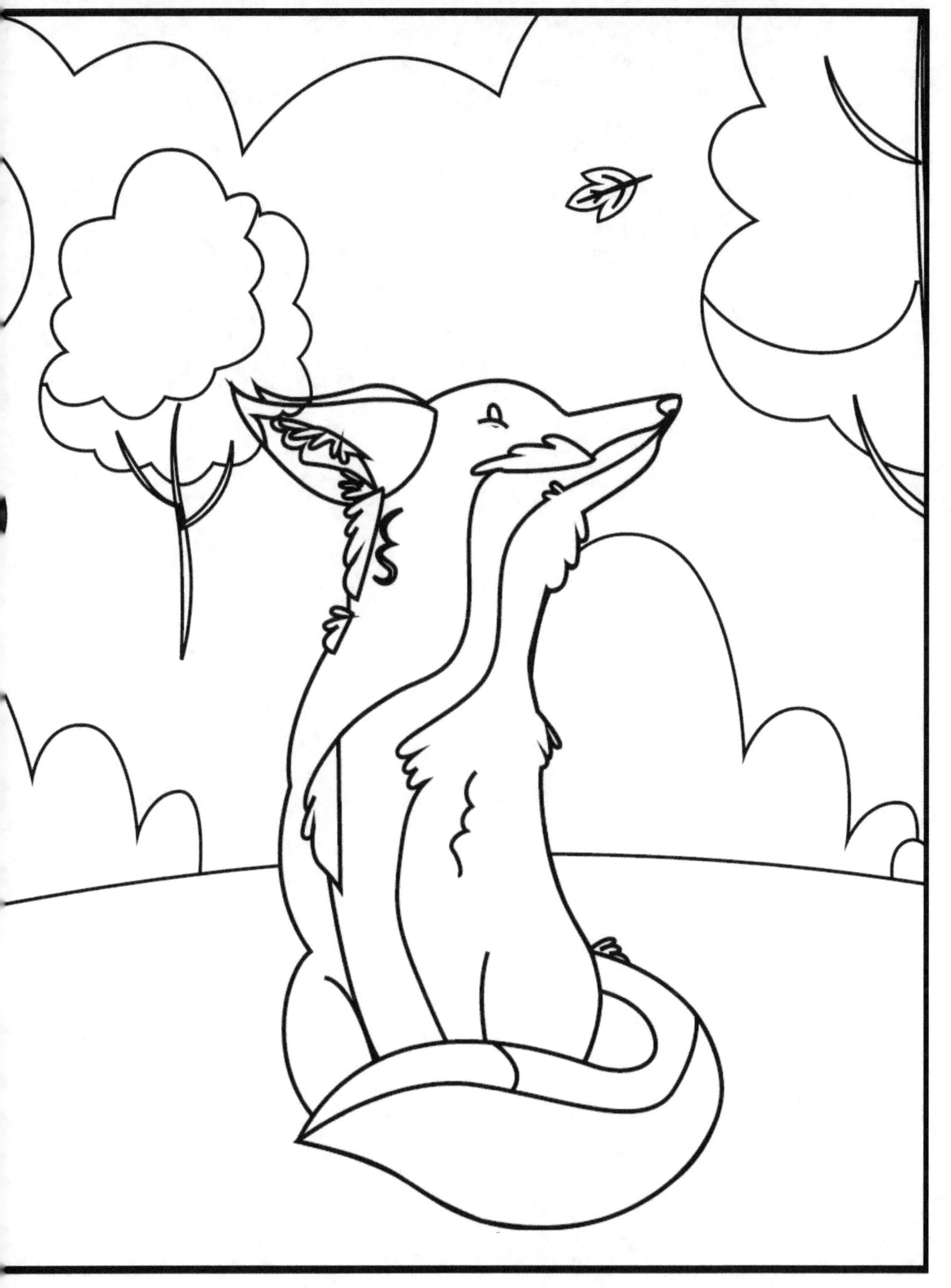

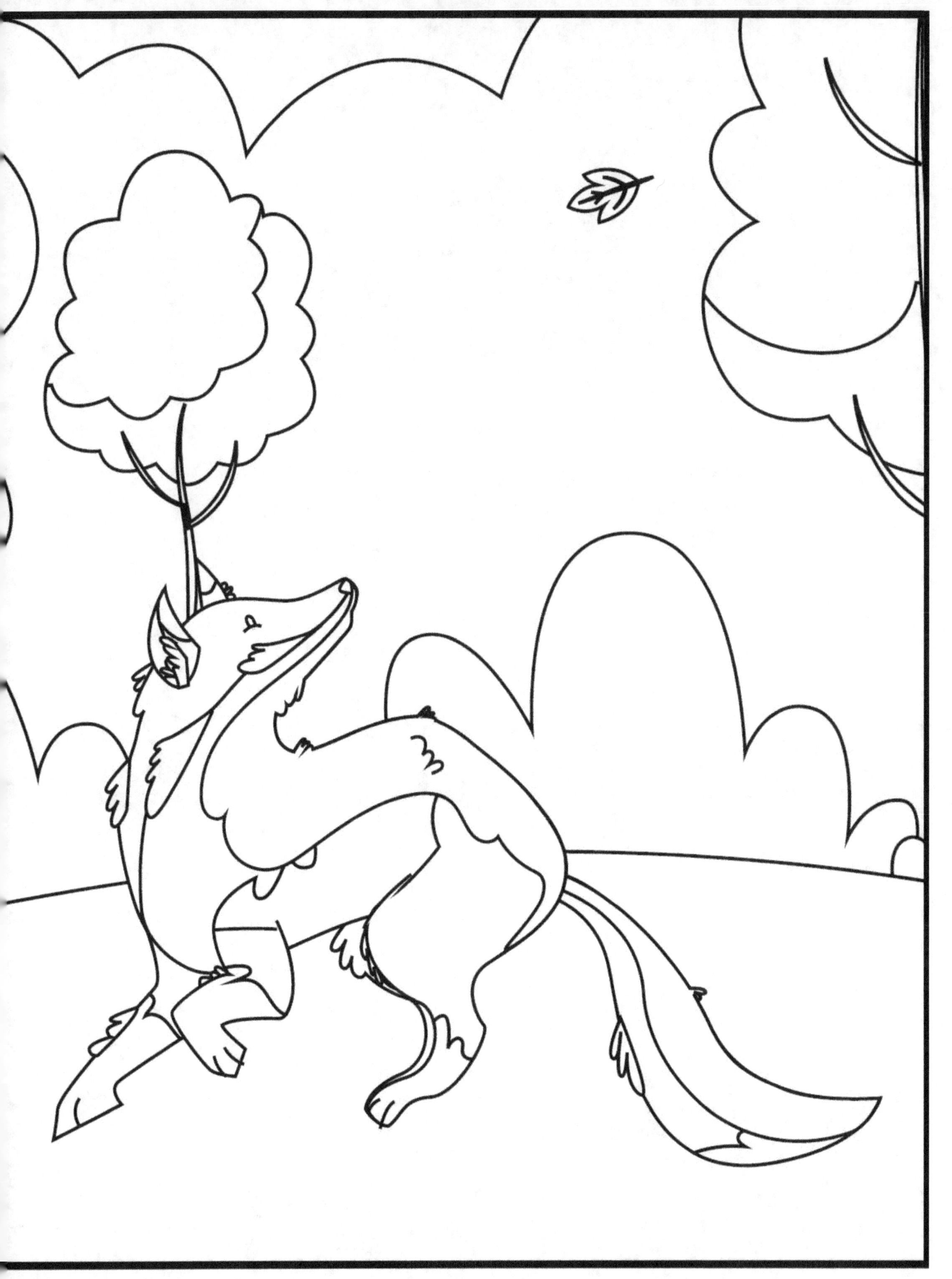

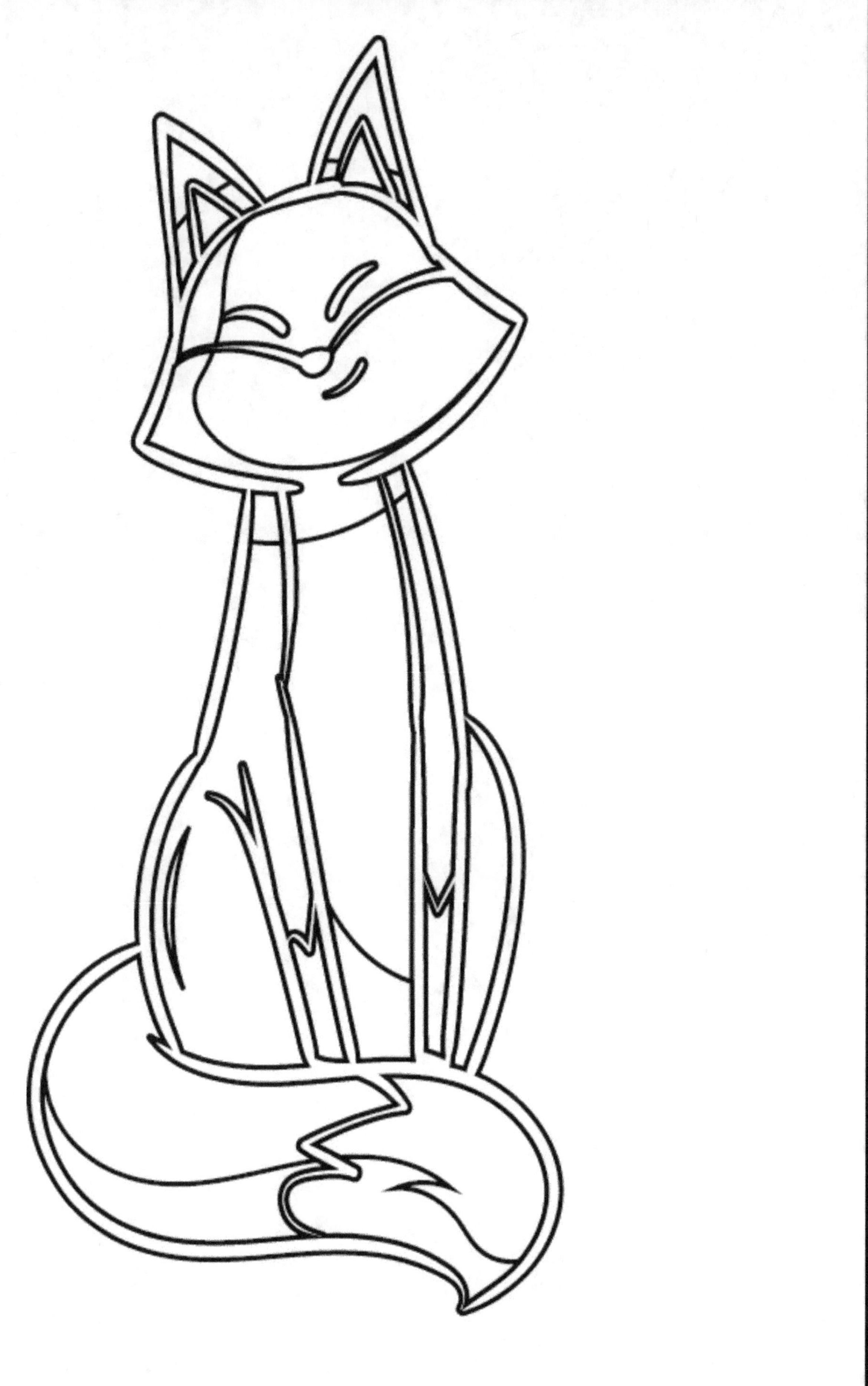

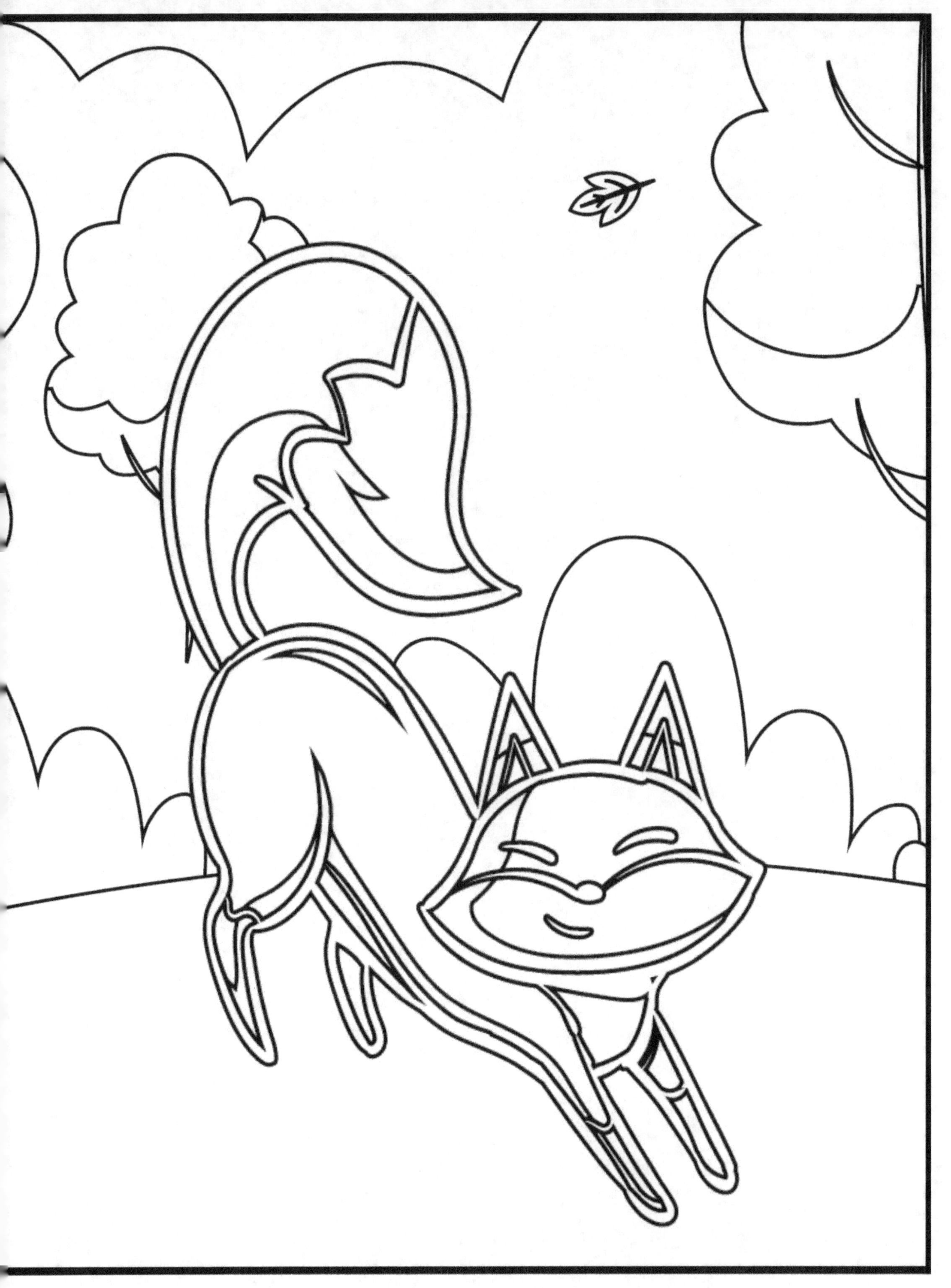

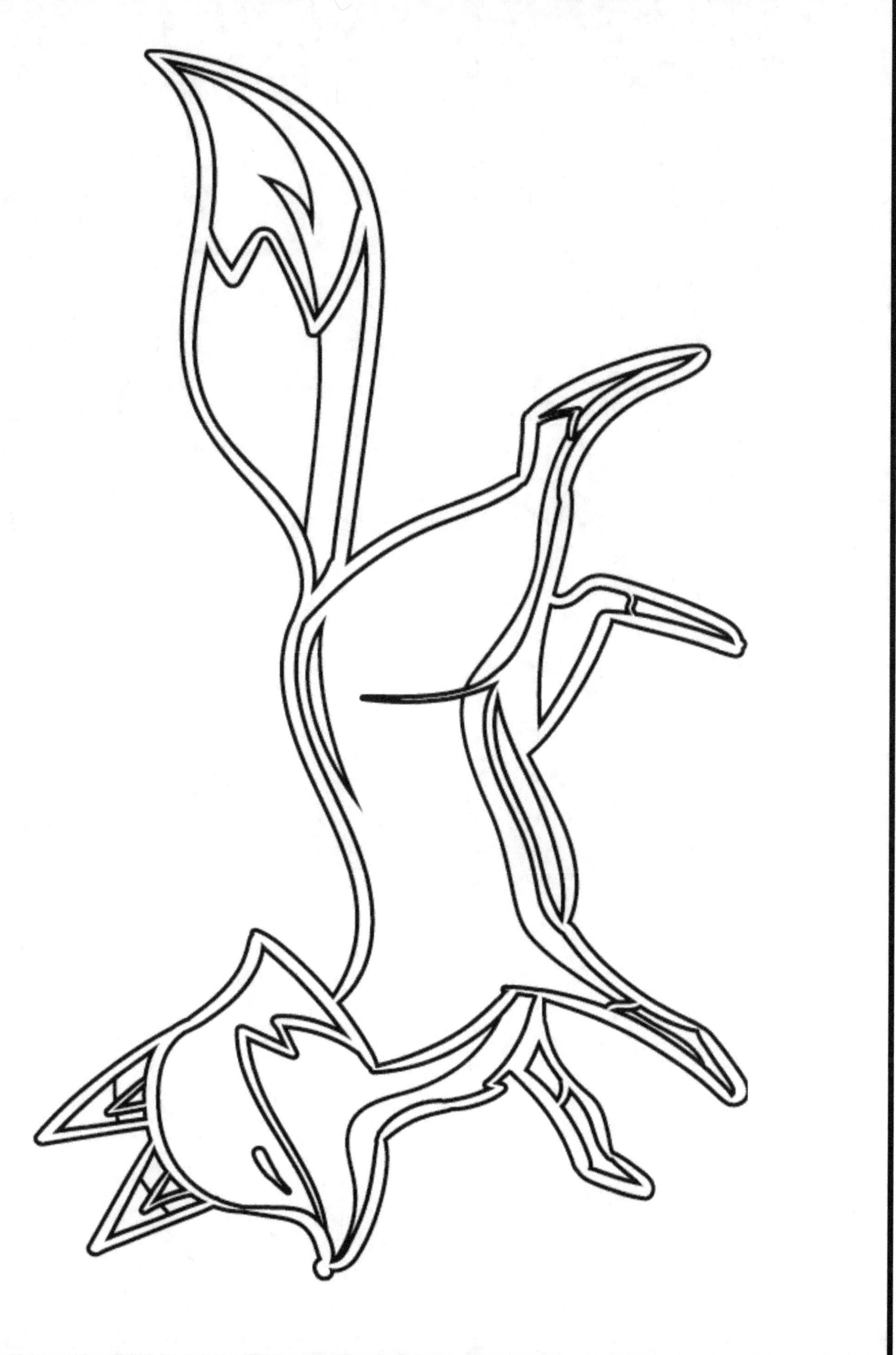

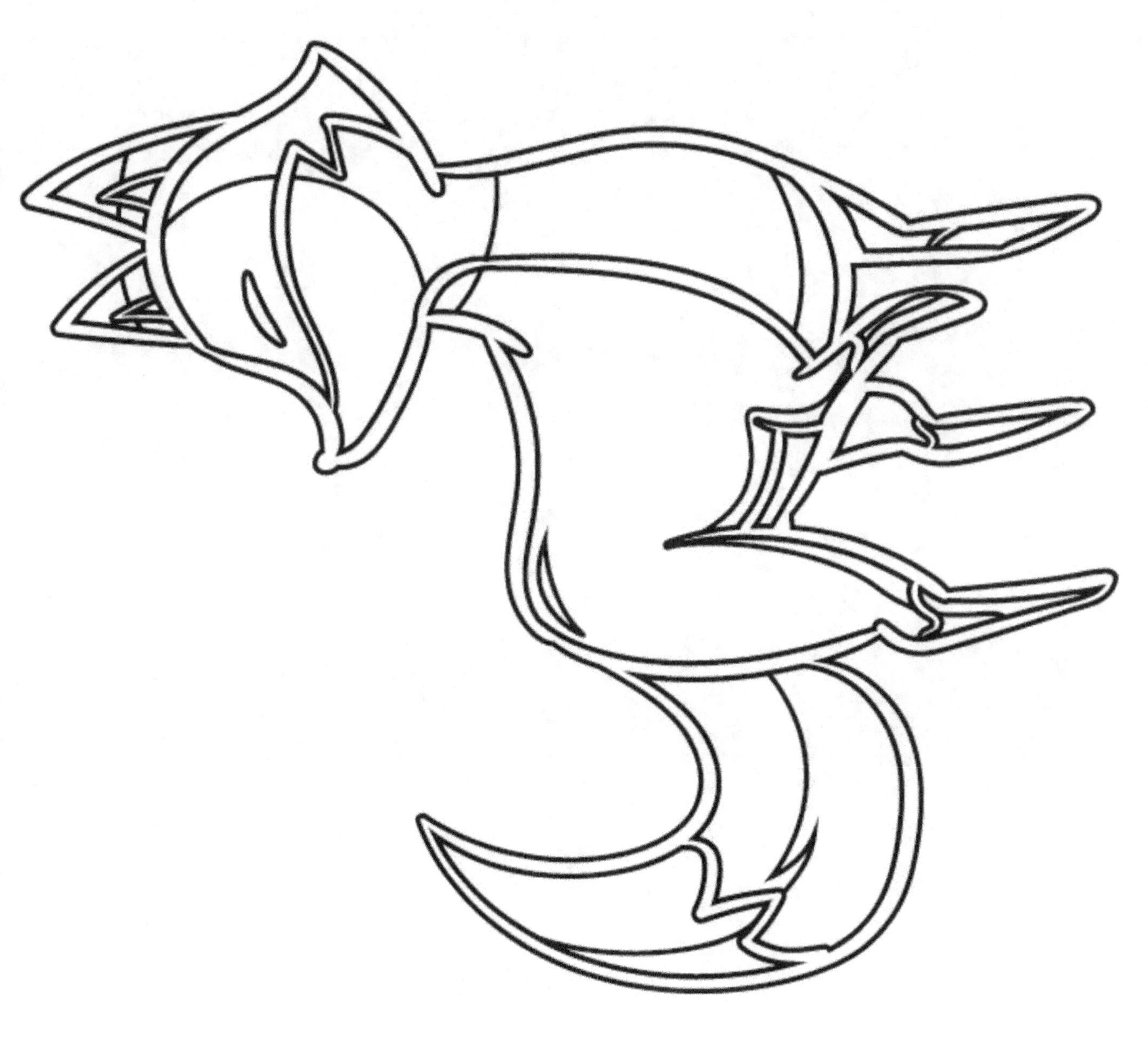

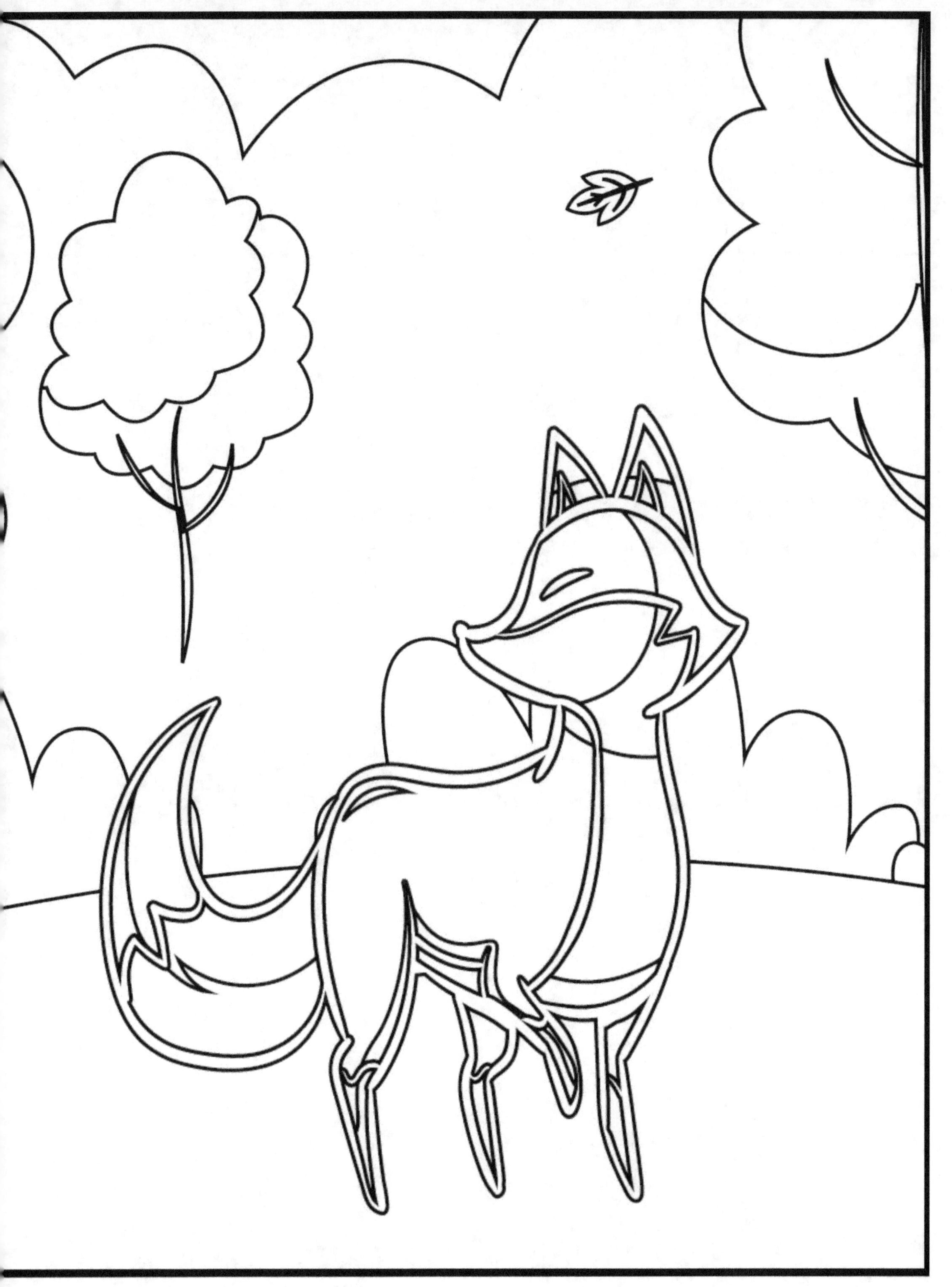

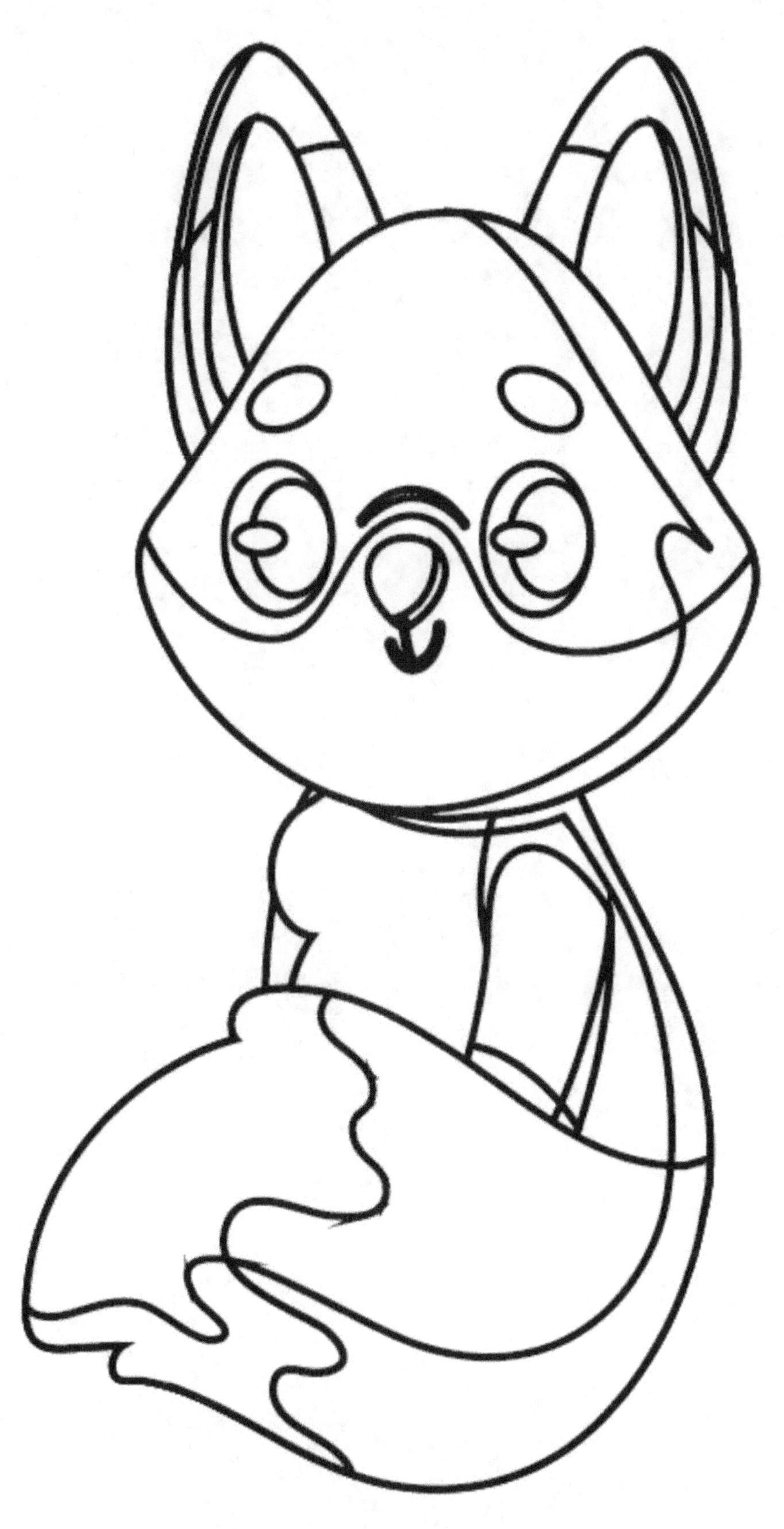

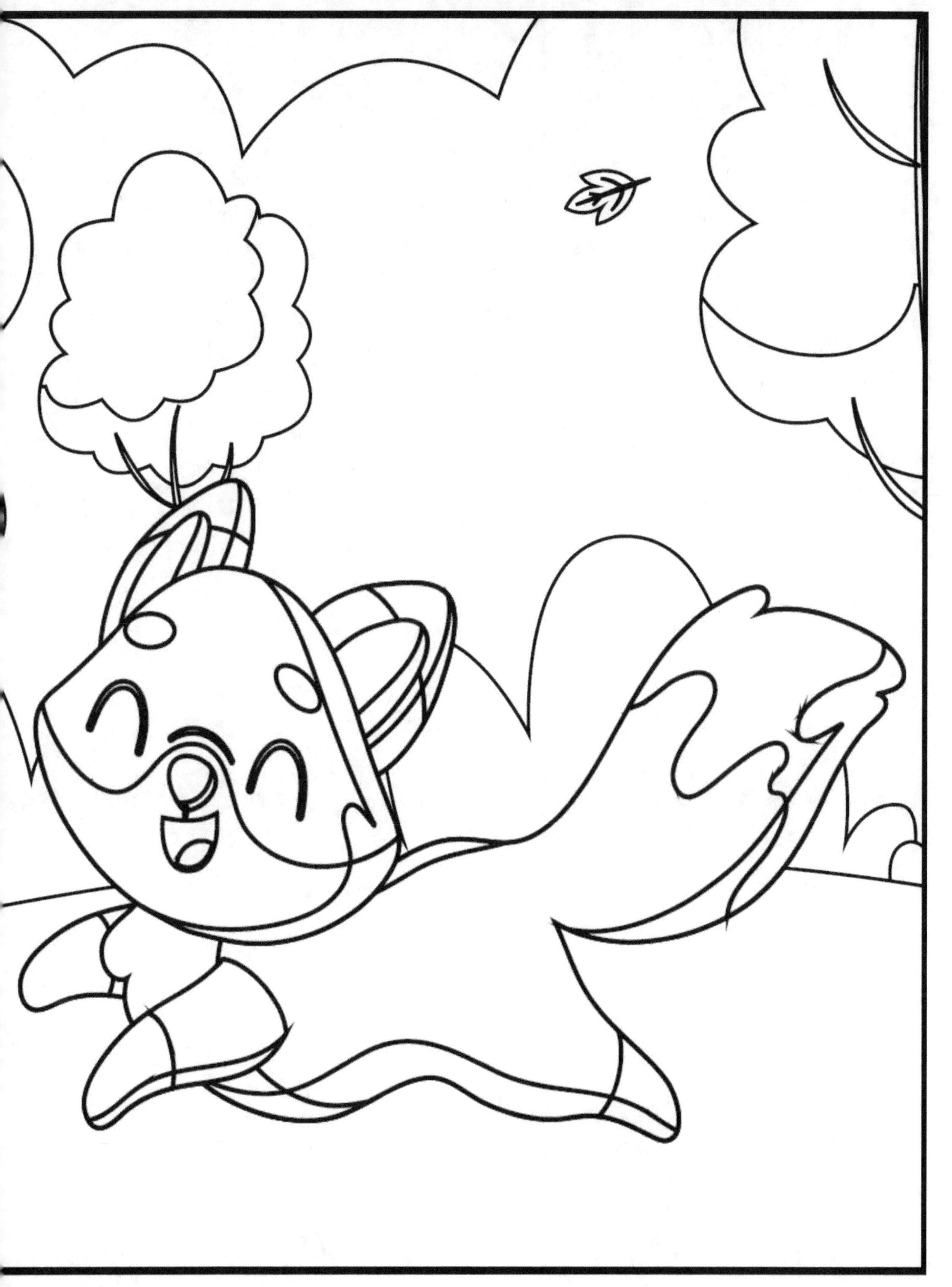

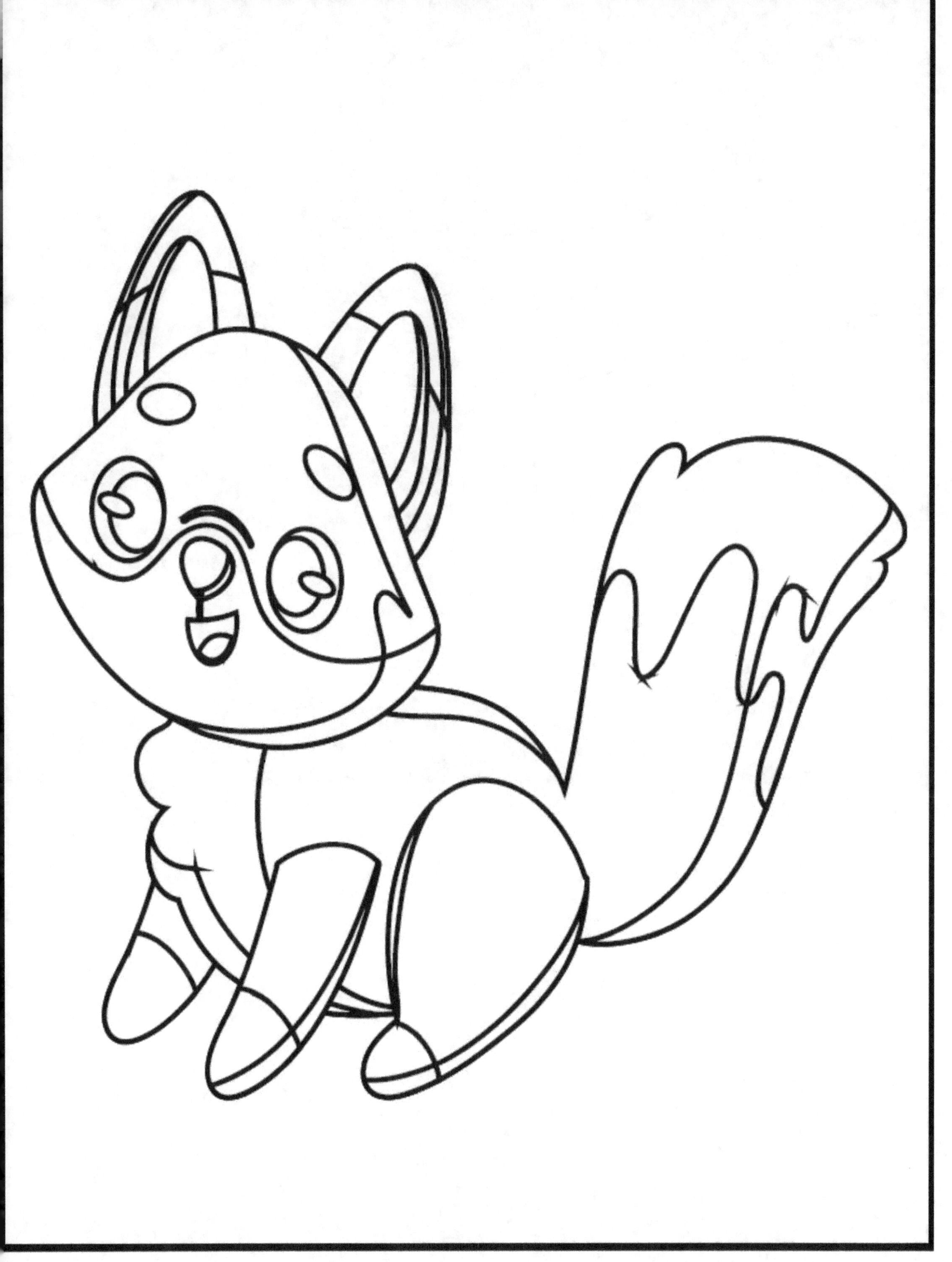

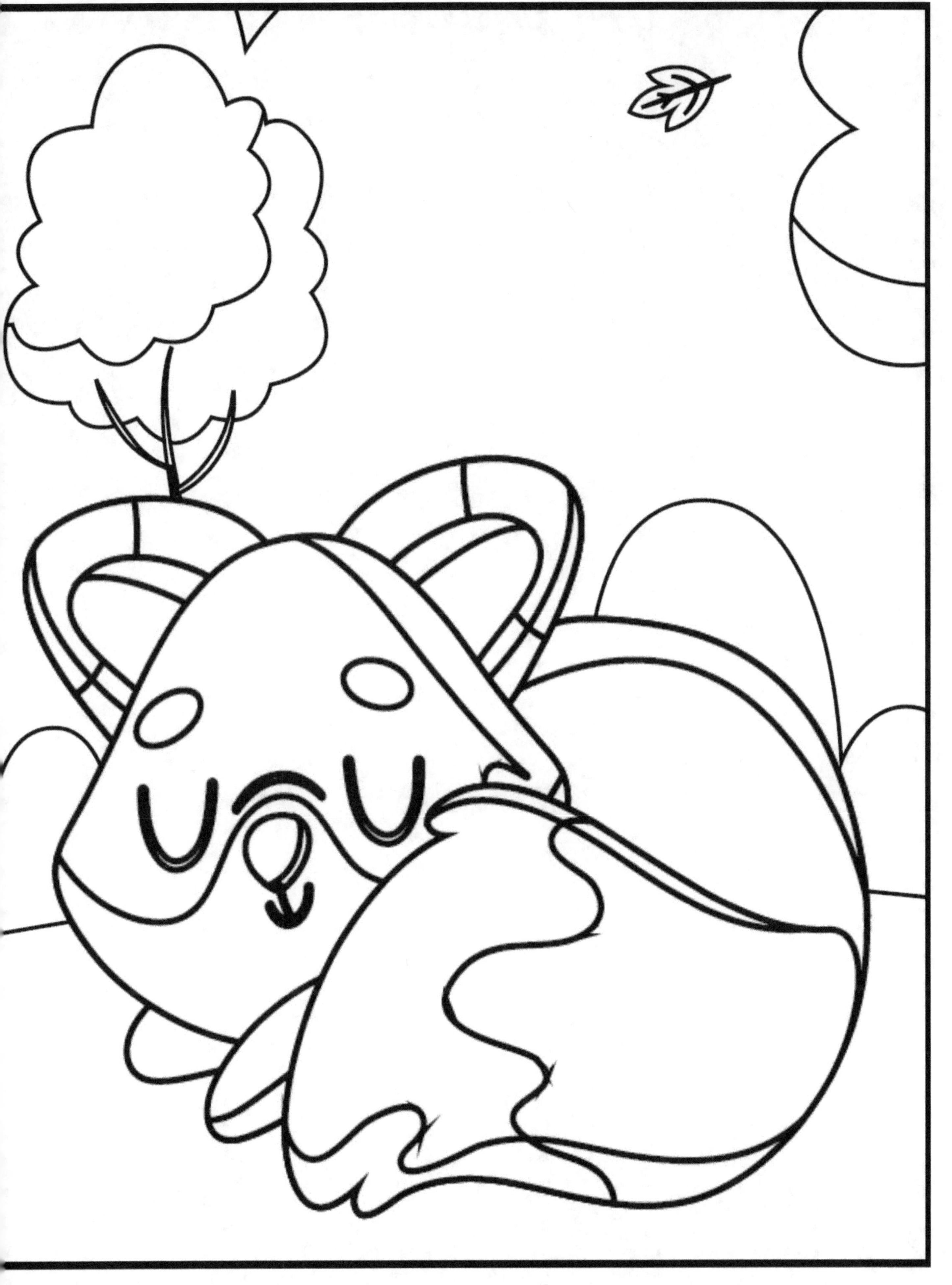

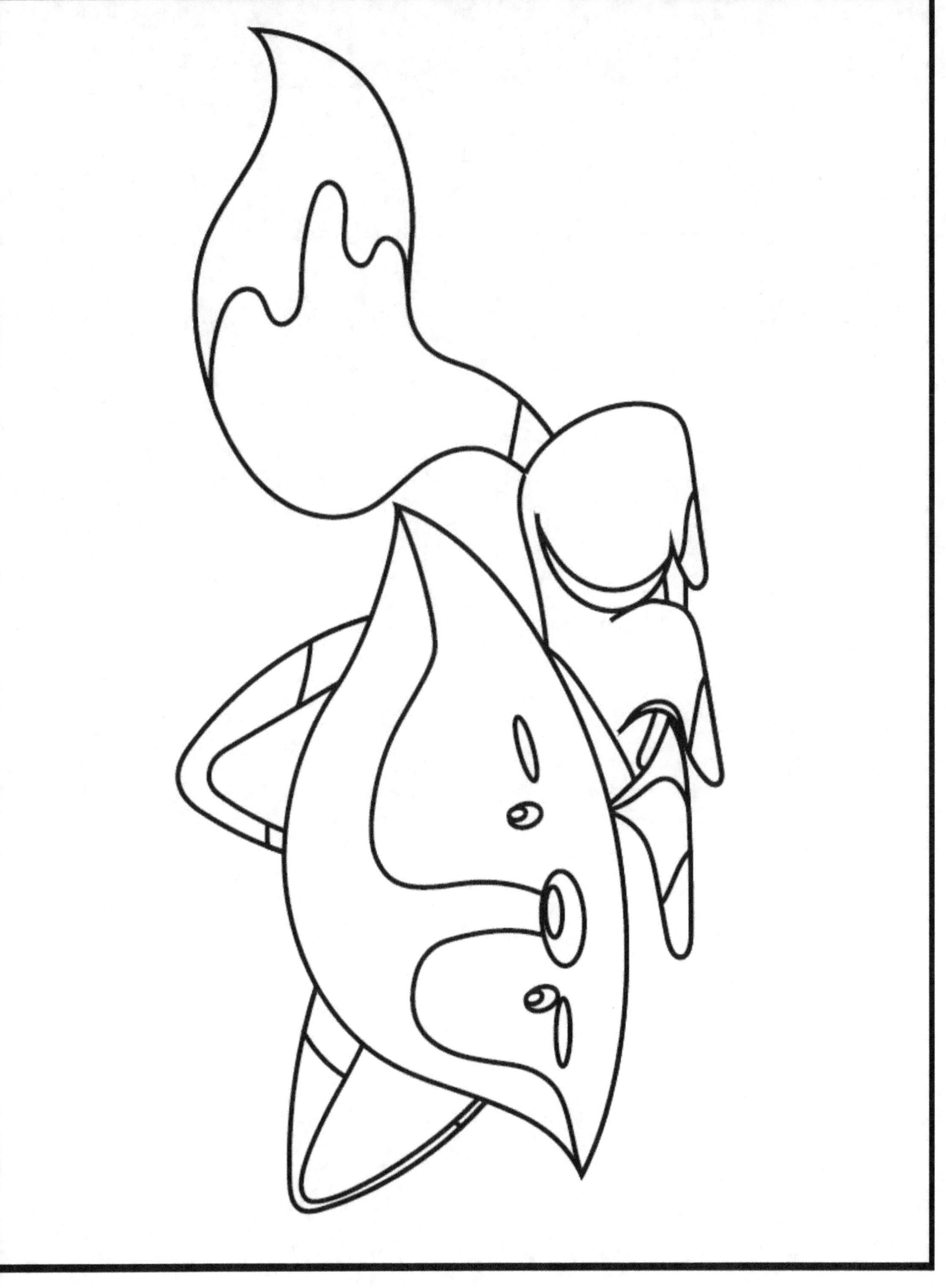

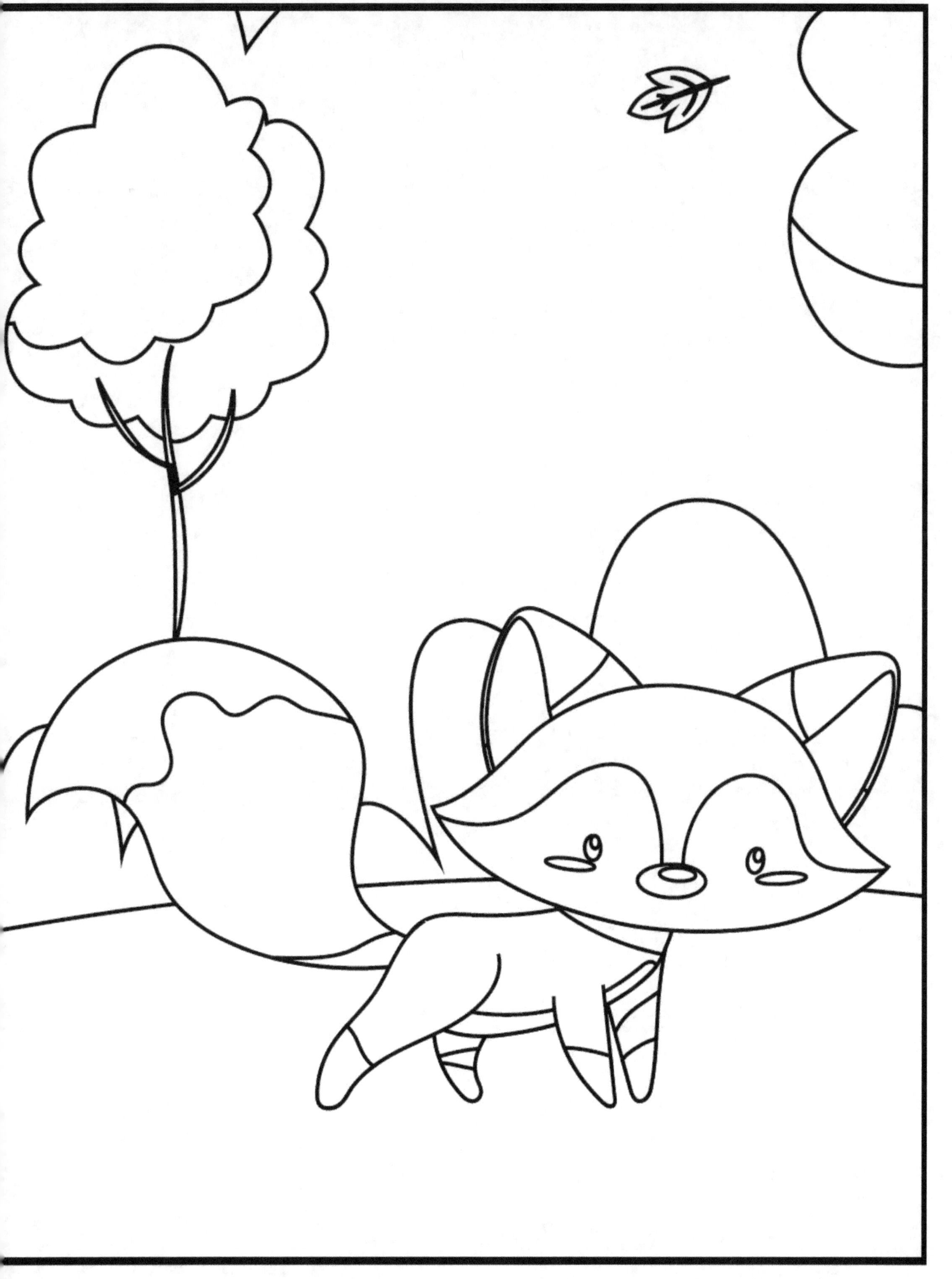